SWEET CUPCAKES
COLORING BOOK

Copyright © 2021 COLORMOOD Books®
All rights reserved.

COLORMOOD
BOOKS®

Sweet Cupkakes Coloring Book

Copyright © 2021 COLORMOOD Books®
All rights reserved.

No part of this publication or the information in it may be quoted
from or reproduced in any form by means such as printing, scanning, photocopying or
otherwise without prior written permission of the copyright holder.

ISBN: 9798702029627

Email: info@colormoodbooks.com

www.colormoodbooks.com

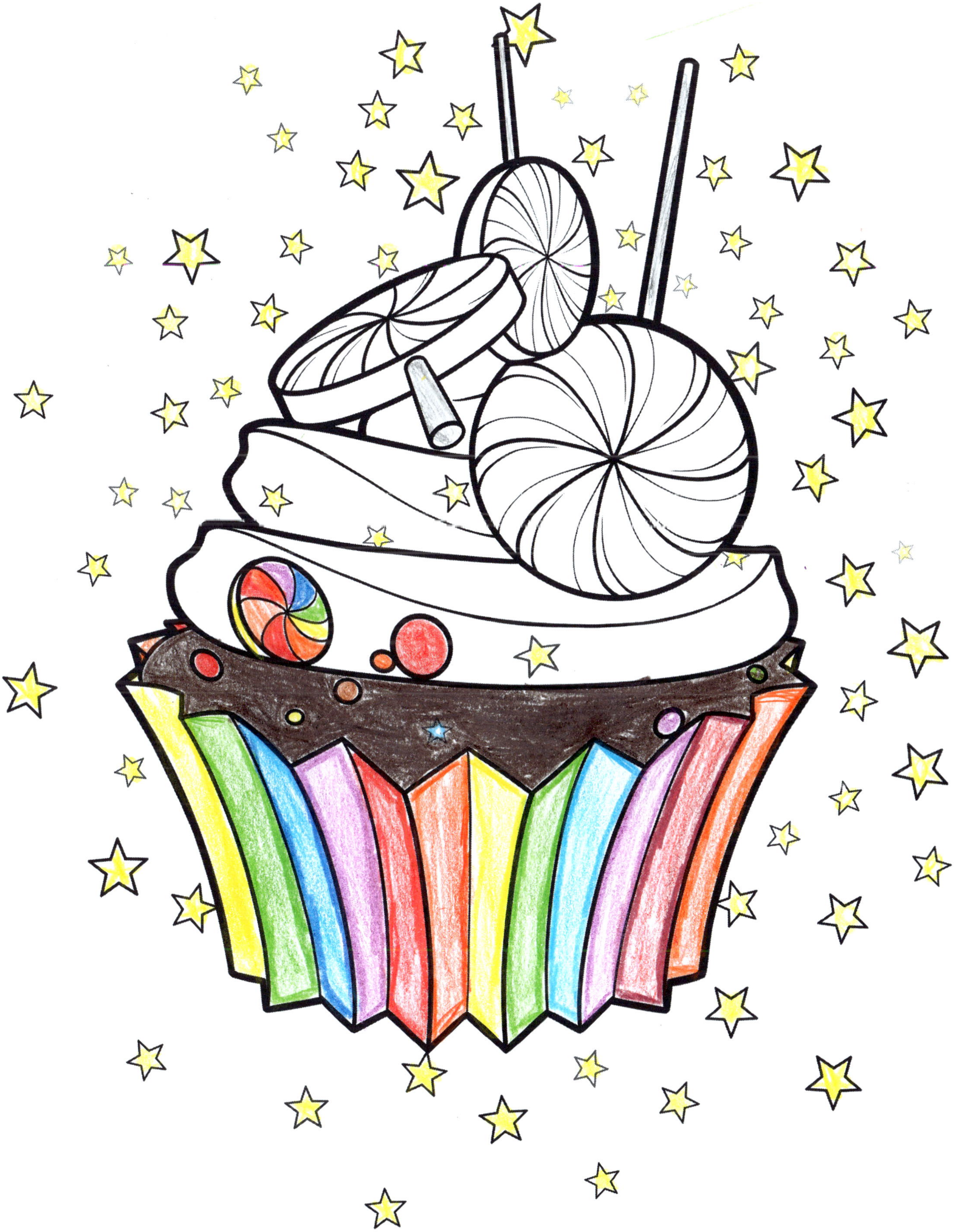

Post your work on Instagram and tag us @colormoodbooks

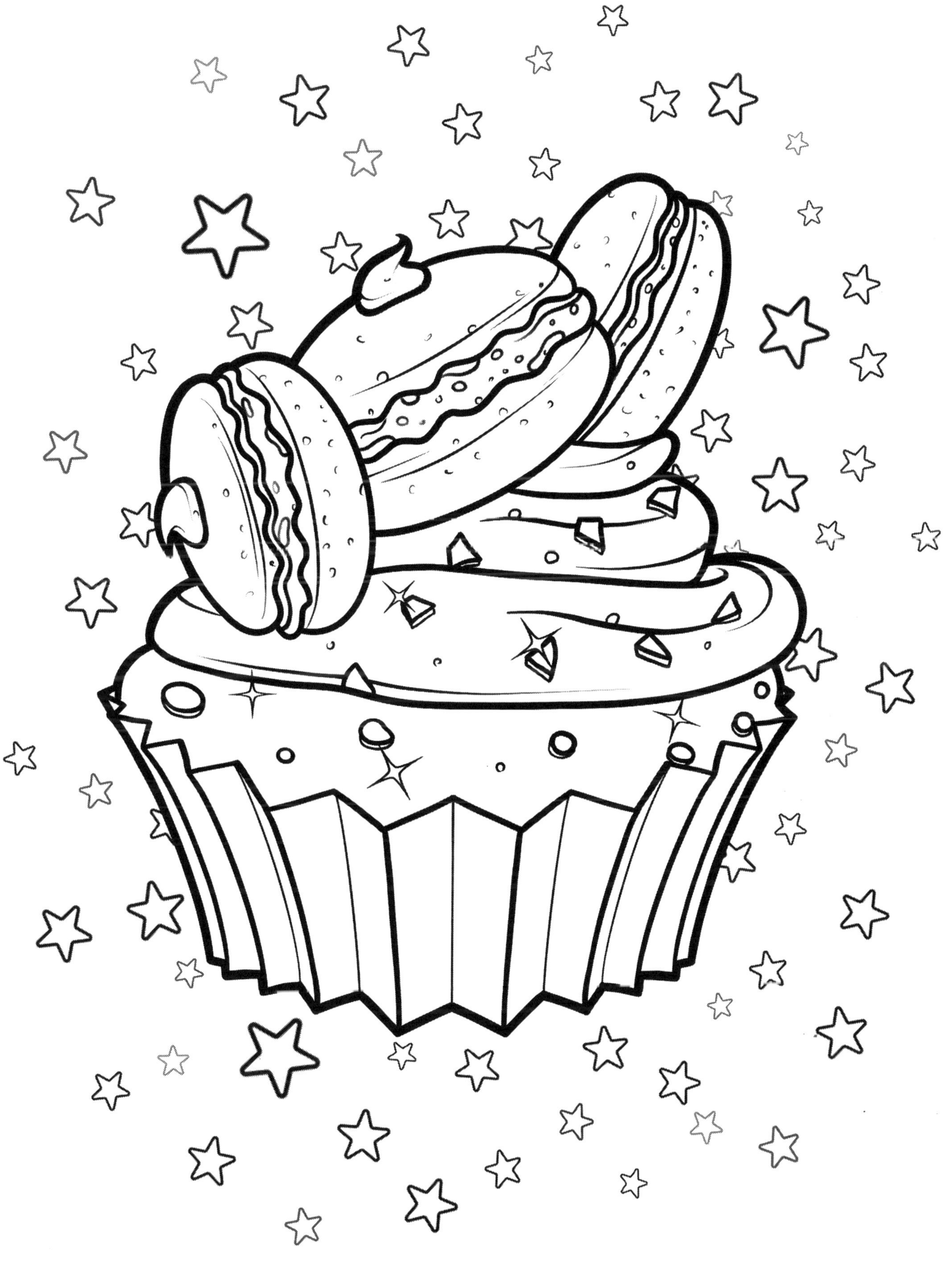

Post your work on Instagram and tag us @colormoodbooks

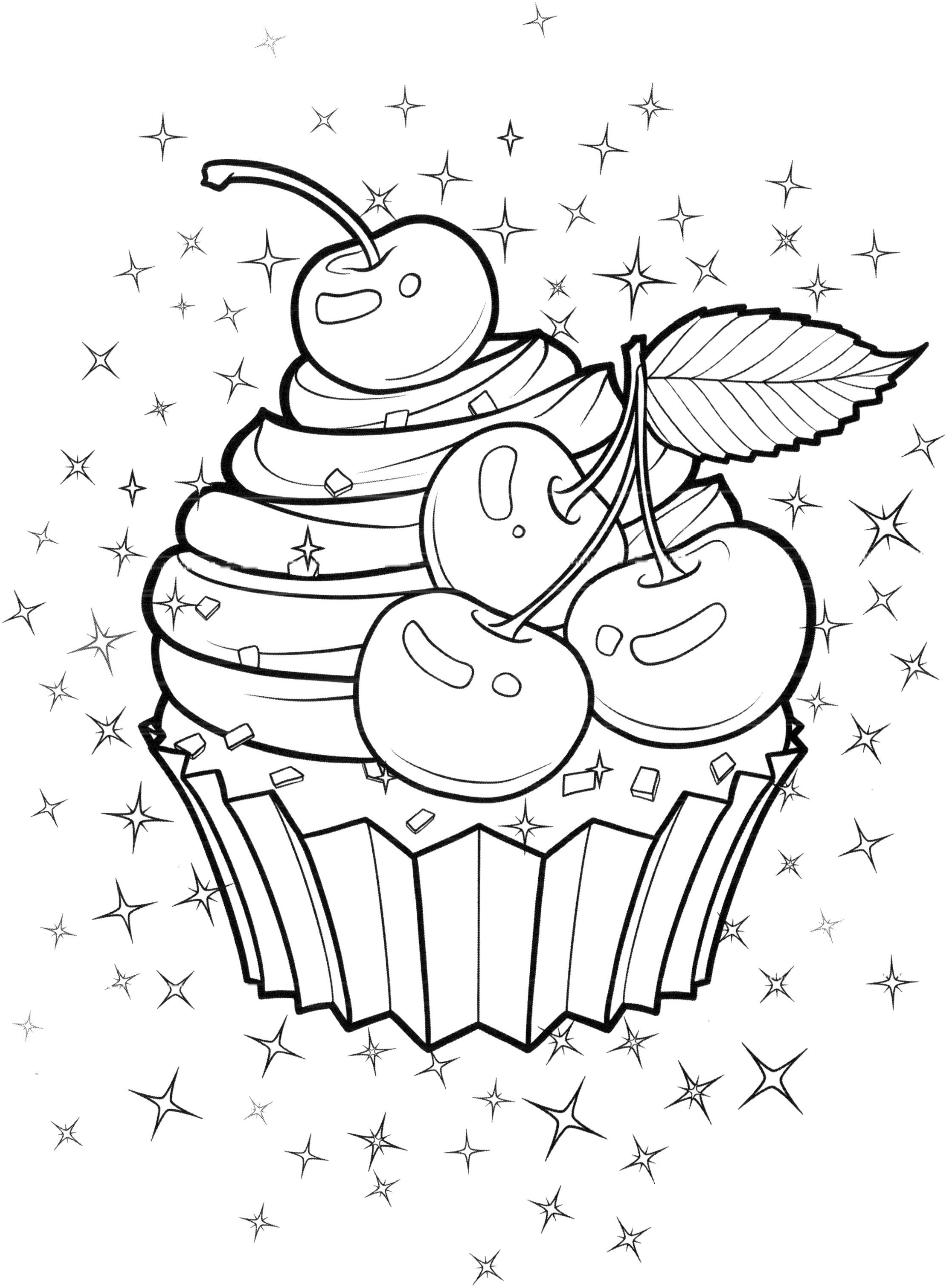

Post your work on Instagram and tag us @colormoodbooks

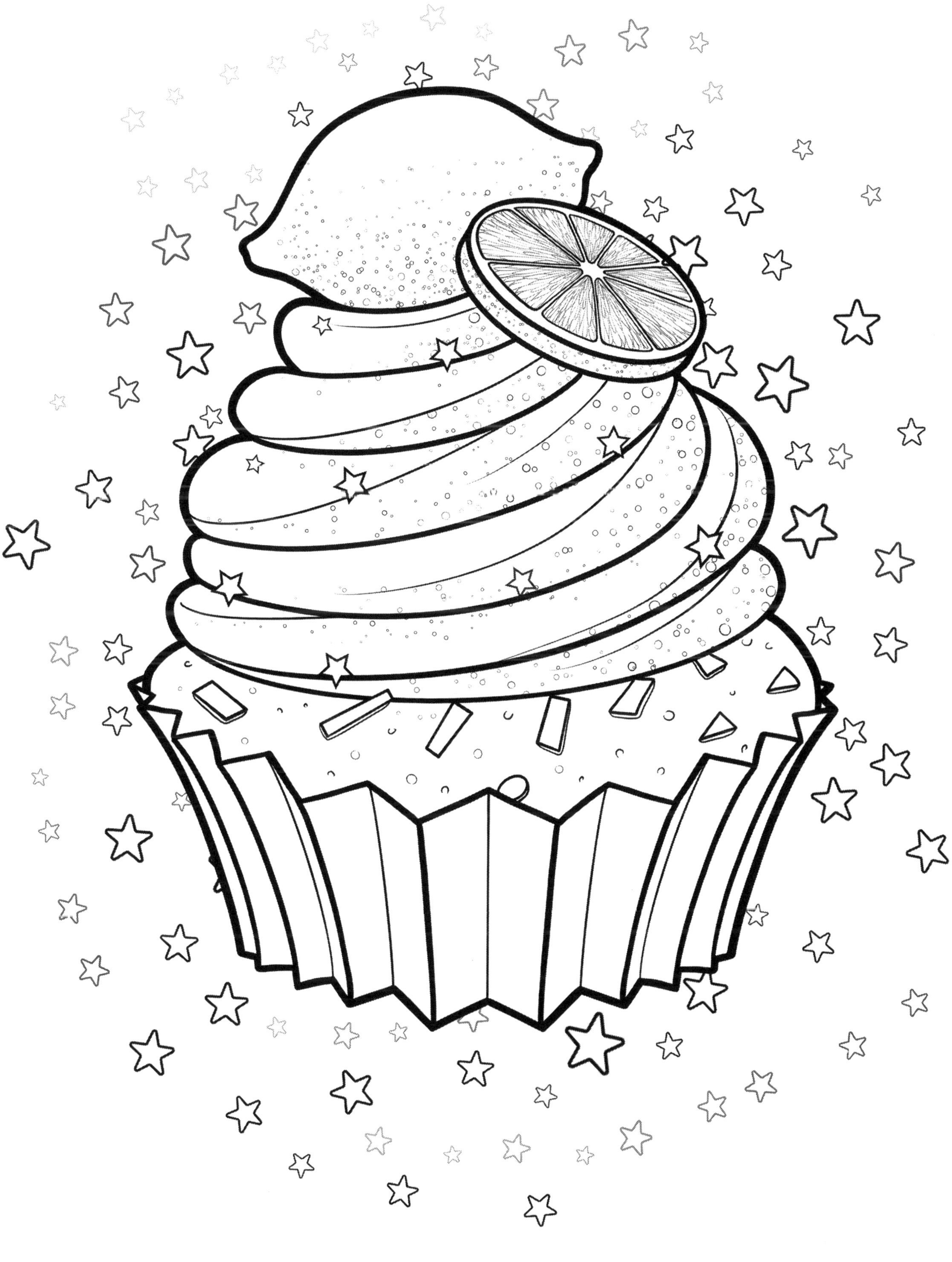

Post your work on Instagram and tag us @colormoodbooks

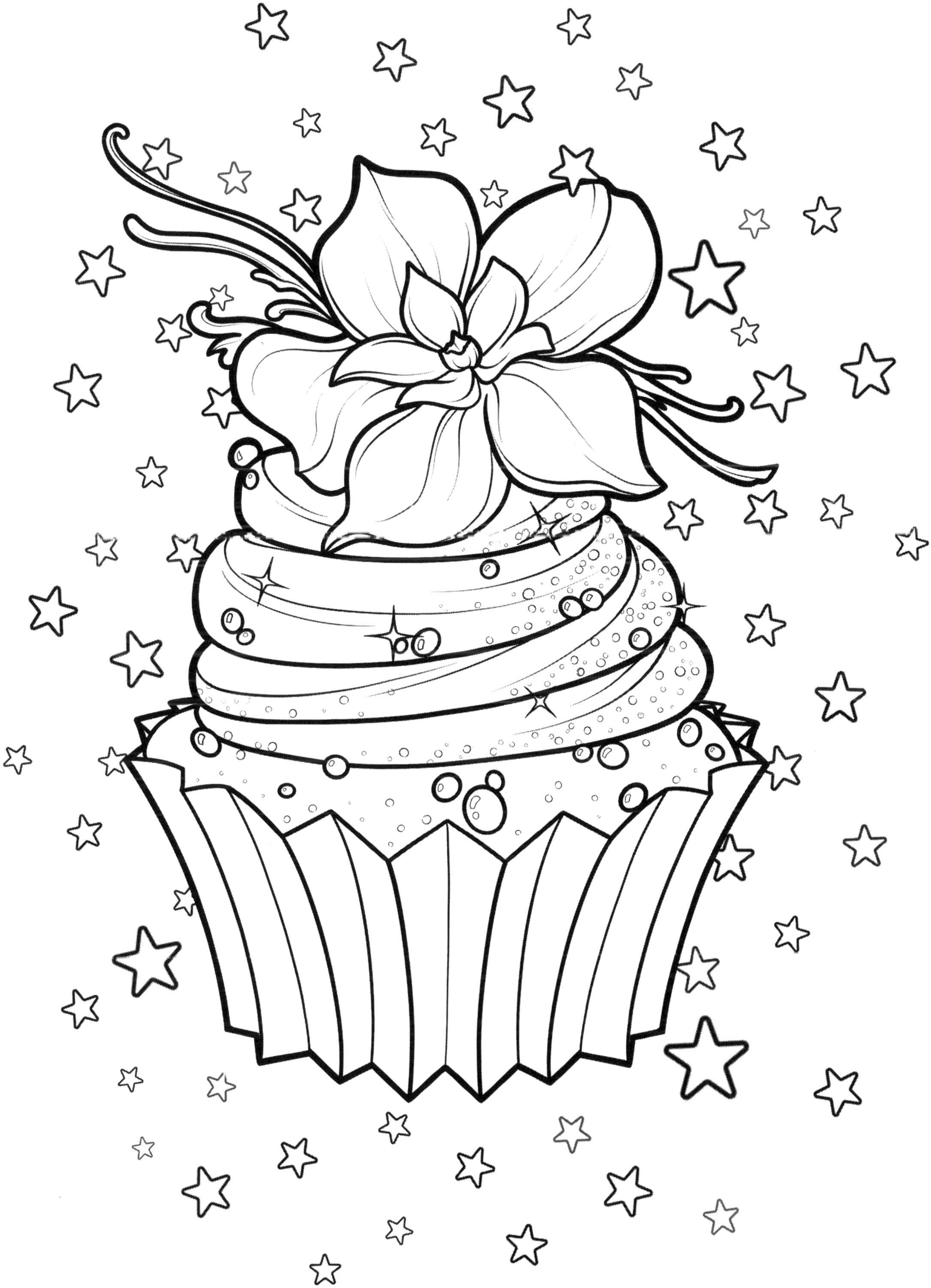

Post your work on Instagram and tag us @colormoodbooks

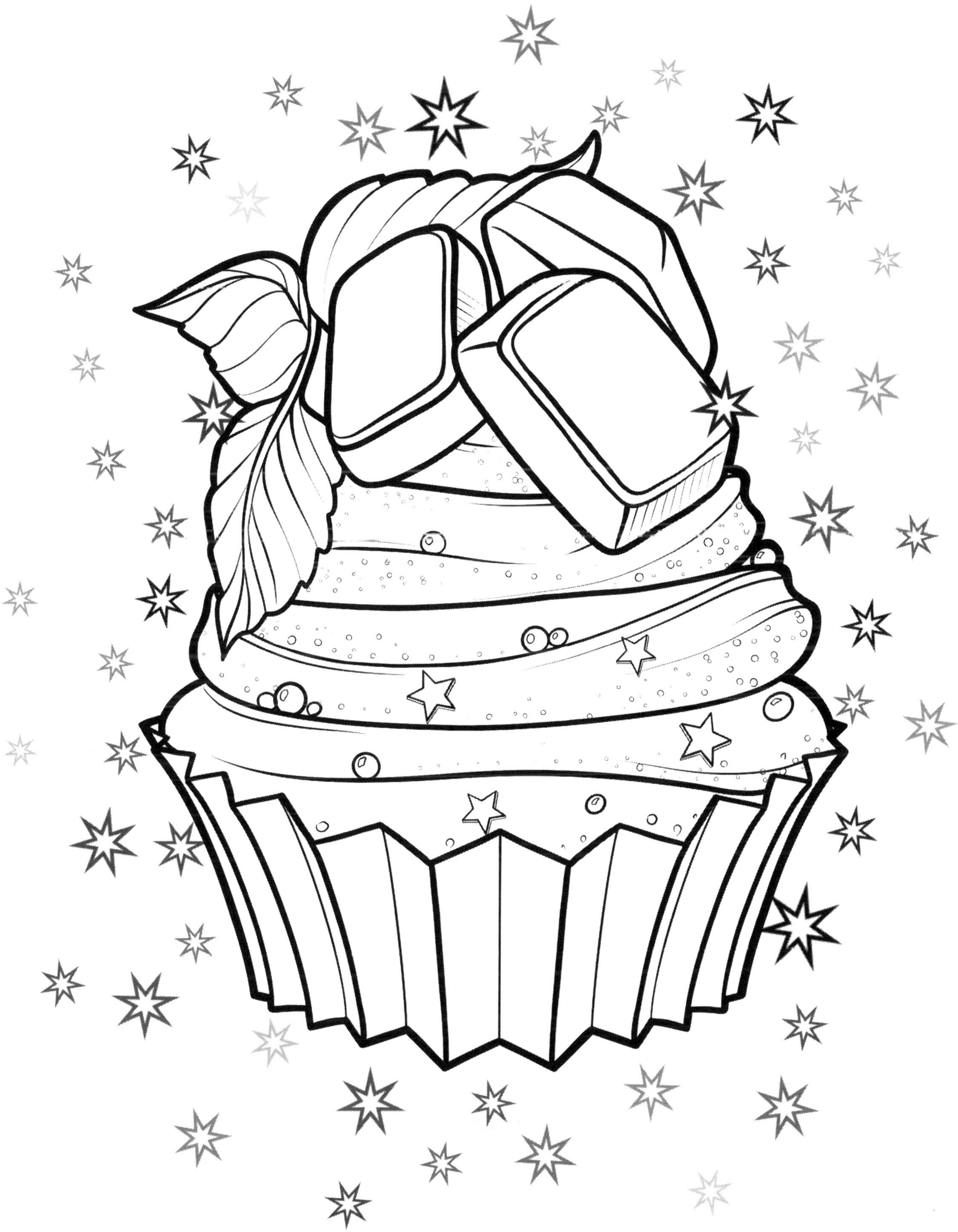

Post your work on Instagram and tag us @colormoodbooks

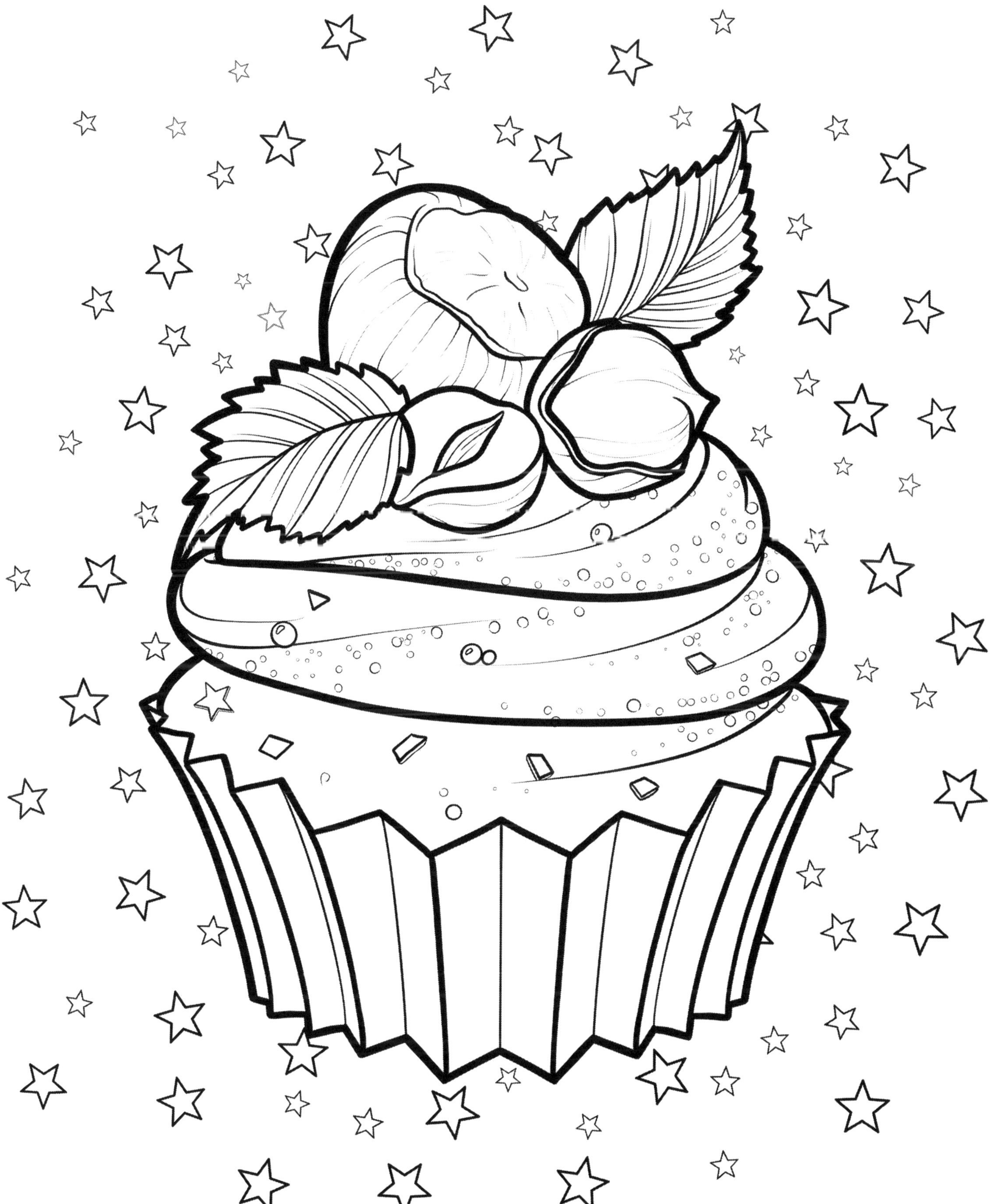

Post your work on Instagram and tag us @colormoodbooks

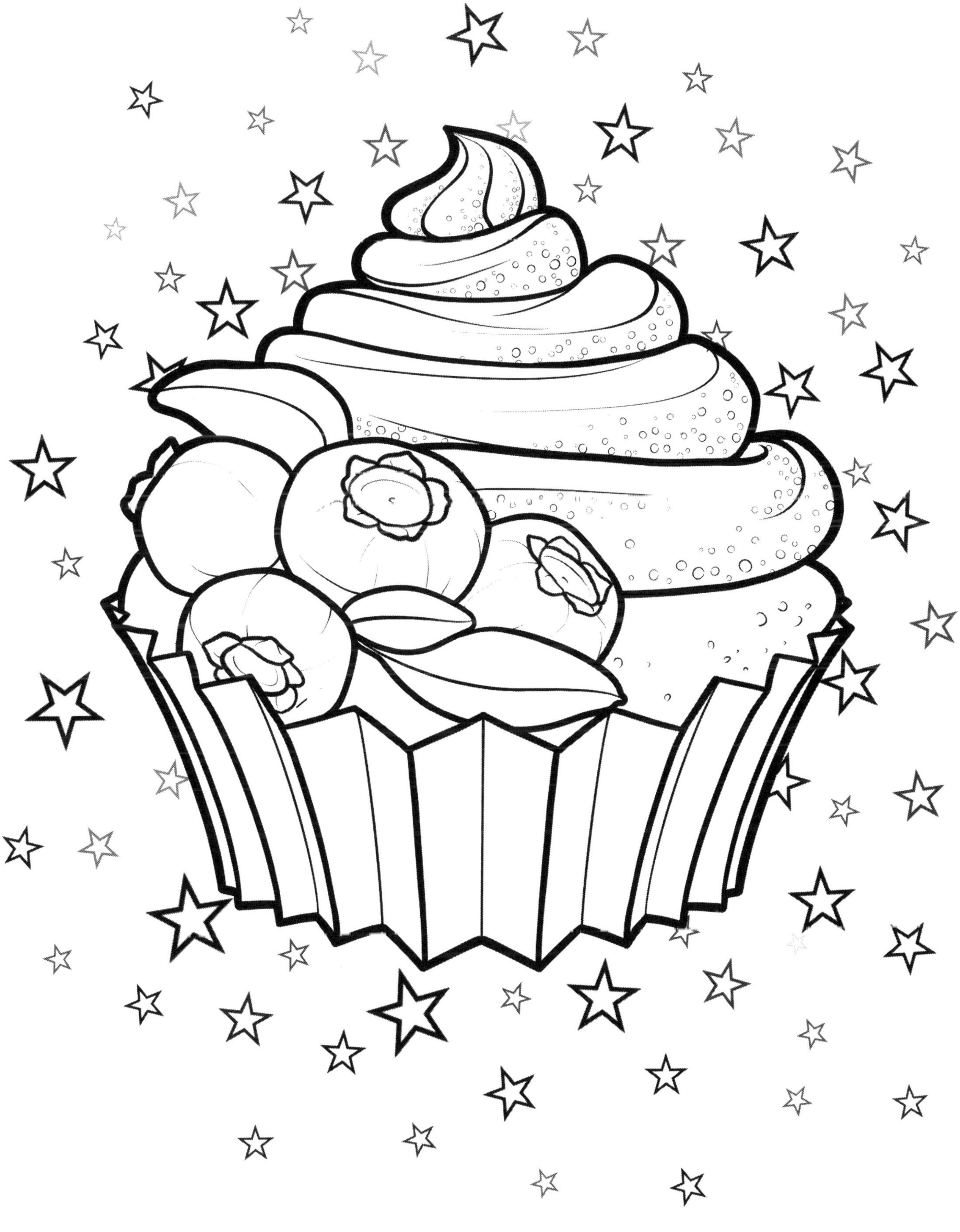

Post your work on Instagram and tag us @colormoodbooks

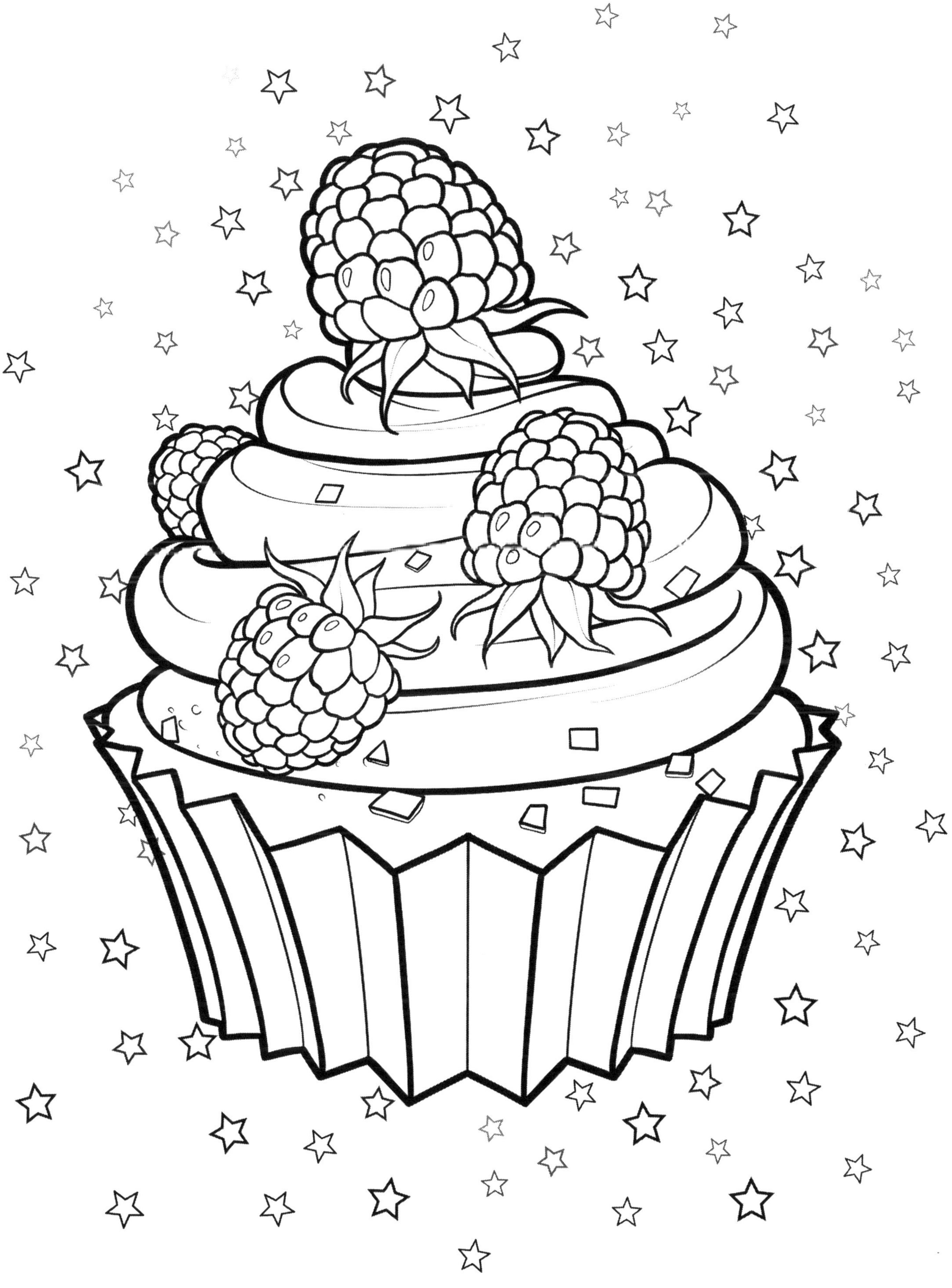

Post your work on Instagram and tag us @colormoodbooks

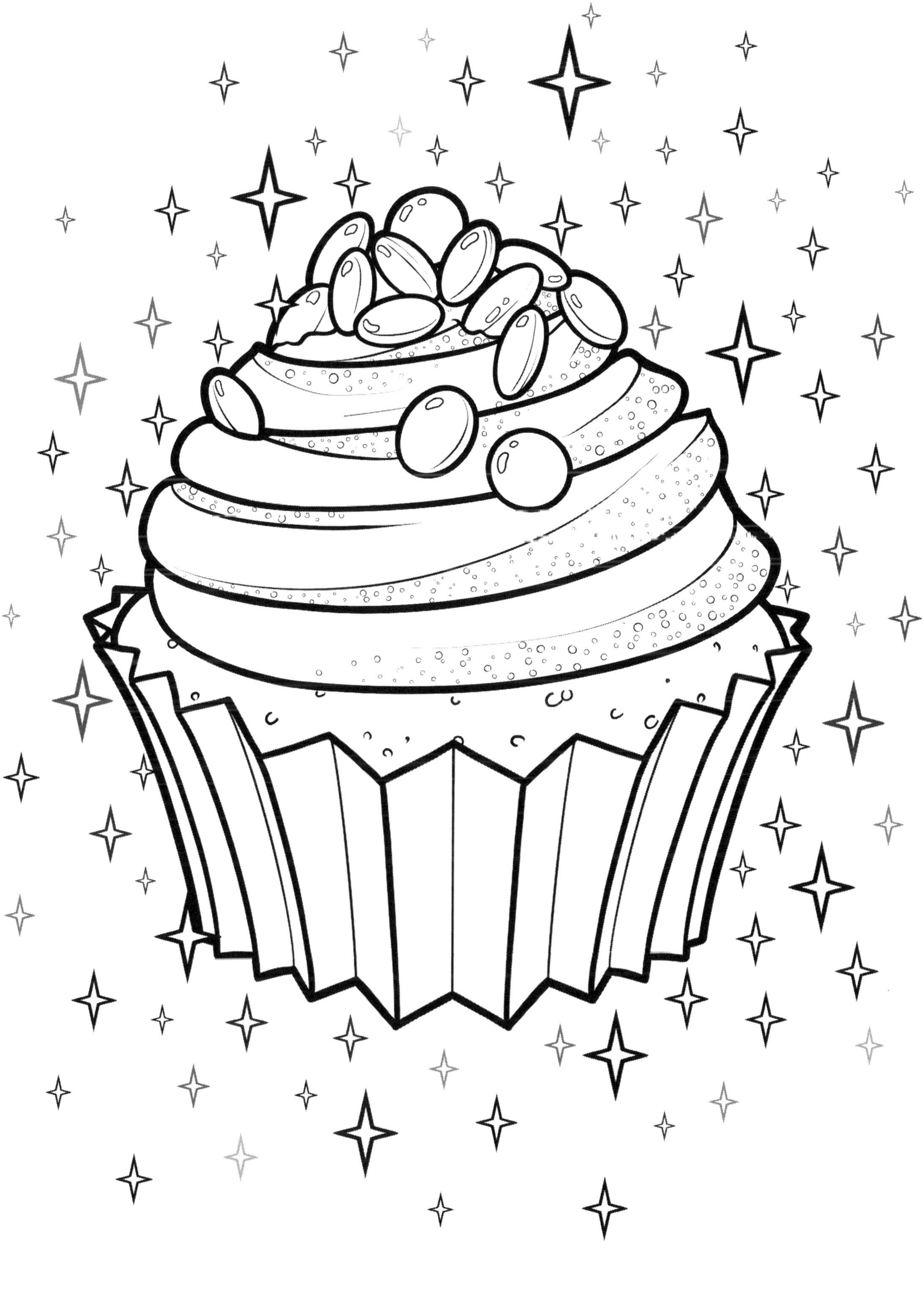

Post your work on Instagram and tag us @colormoodbooks

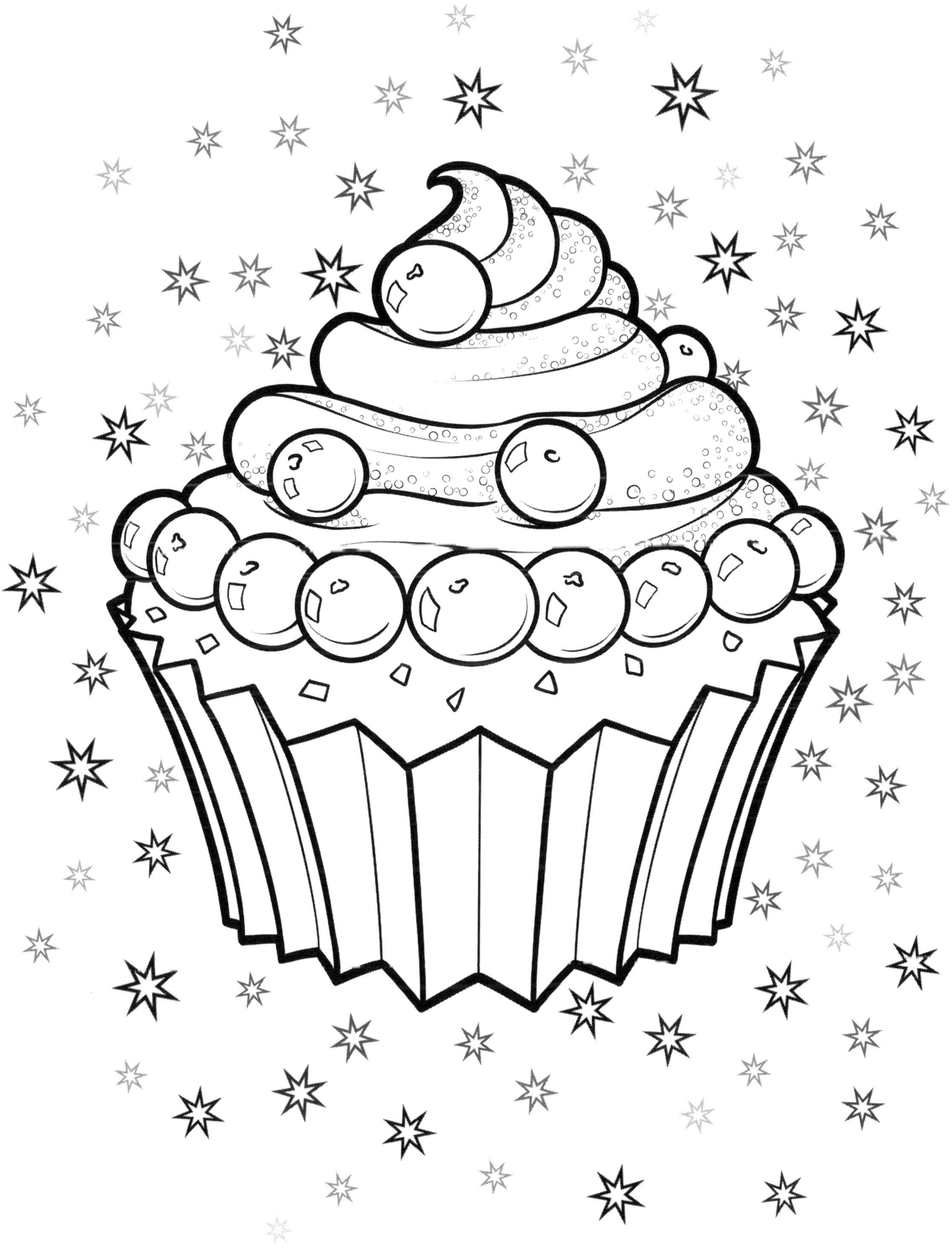

Post your work on Instagram and tag us @colormoodbooks

Post your work on Instagram and tag us @colormoodbooks

Post your work on Instagram and tag us @colormoodbooks

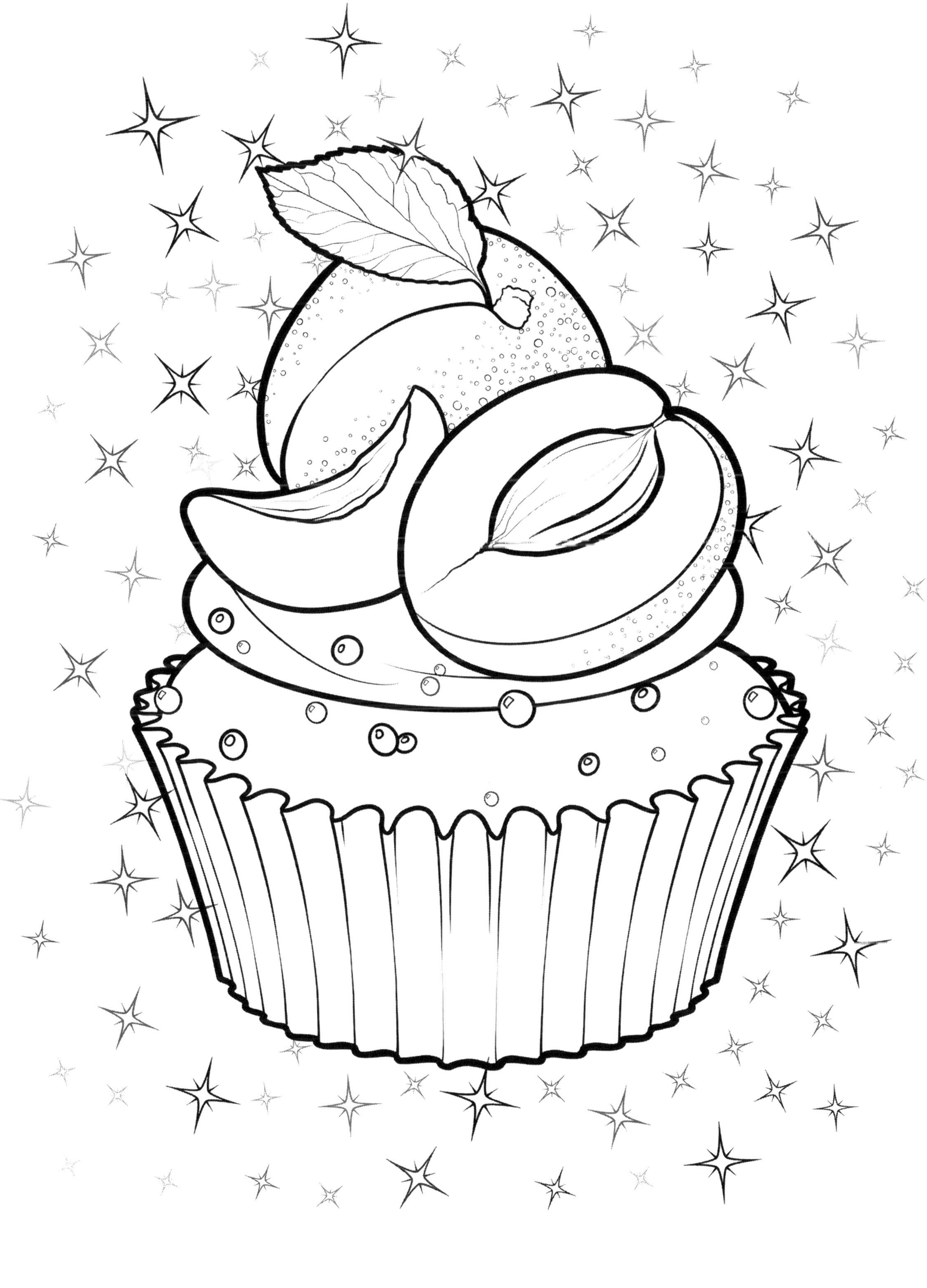

Post your work on Instagram and tag us @colormoodbooks

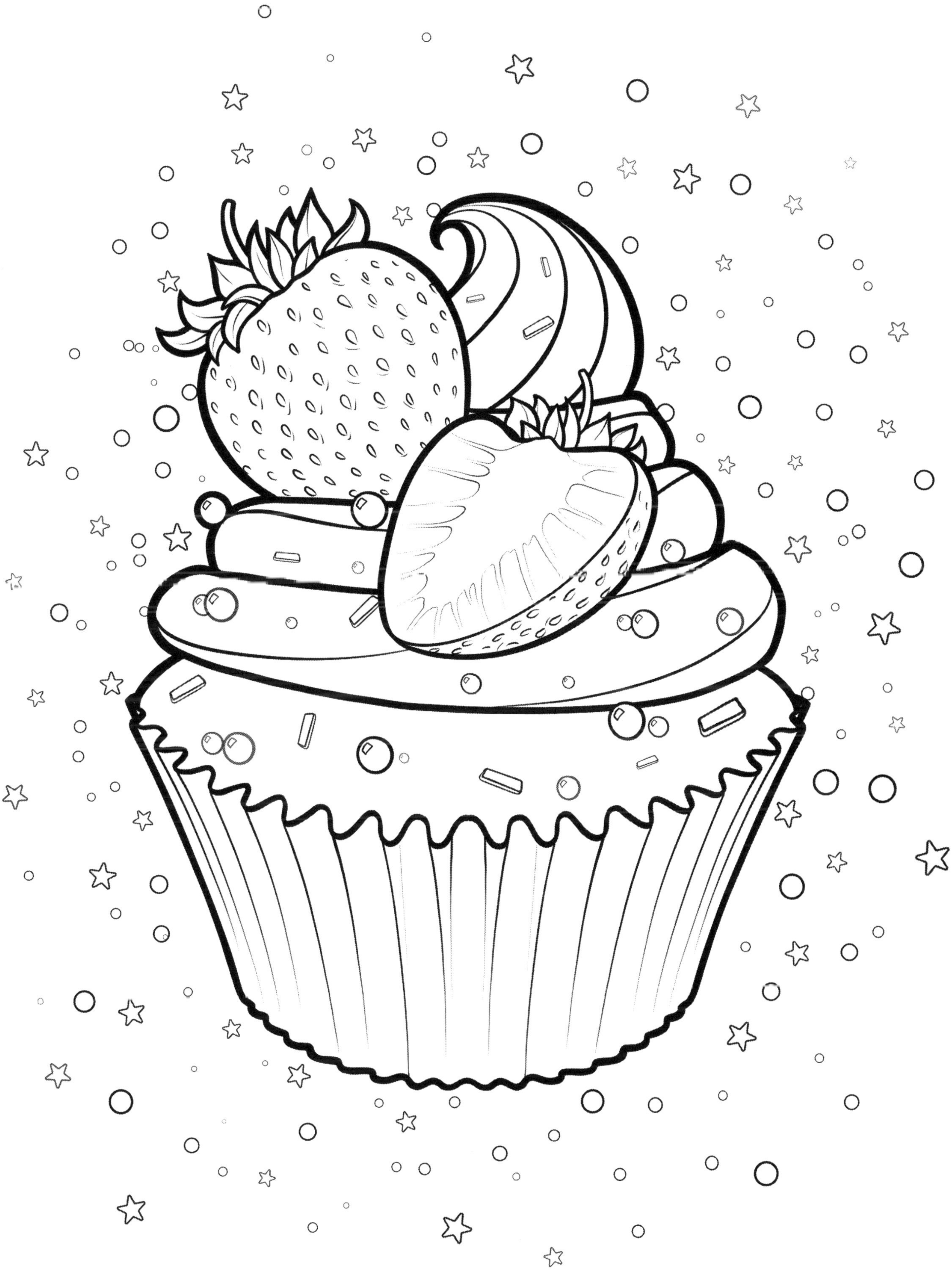

Post your work on Instagram and tag us @colormoodbooks

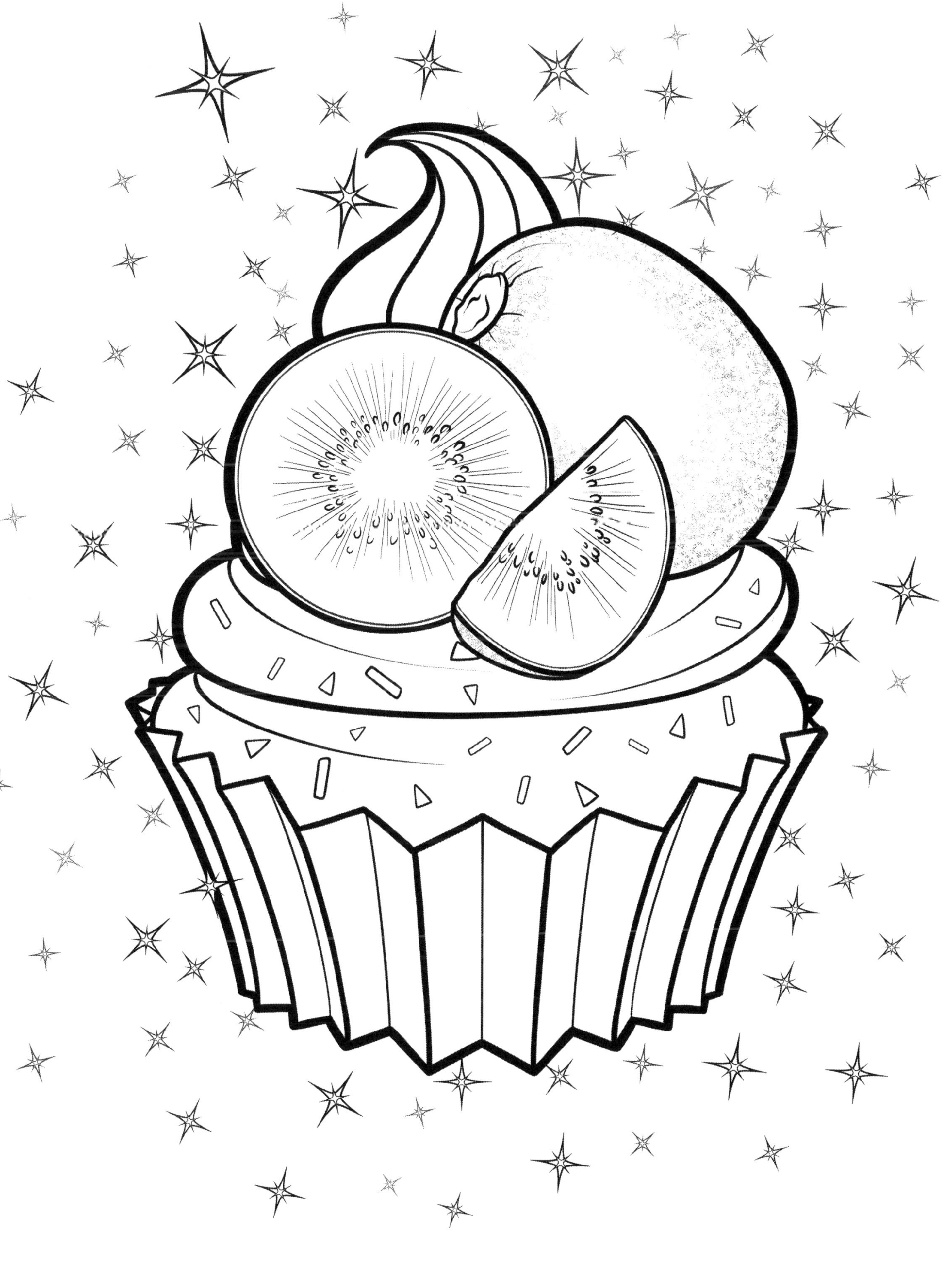

Post your work on Instagram and tag us @colormoodbooks

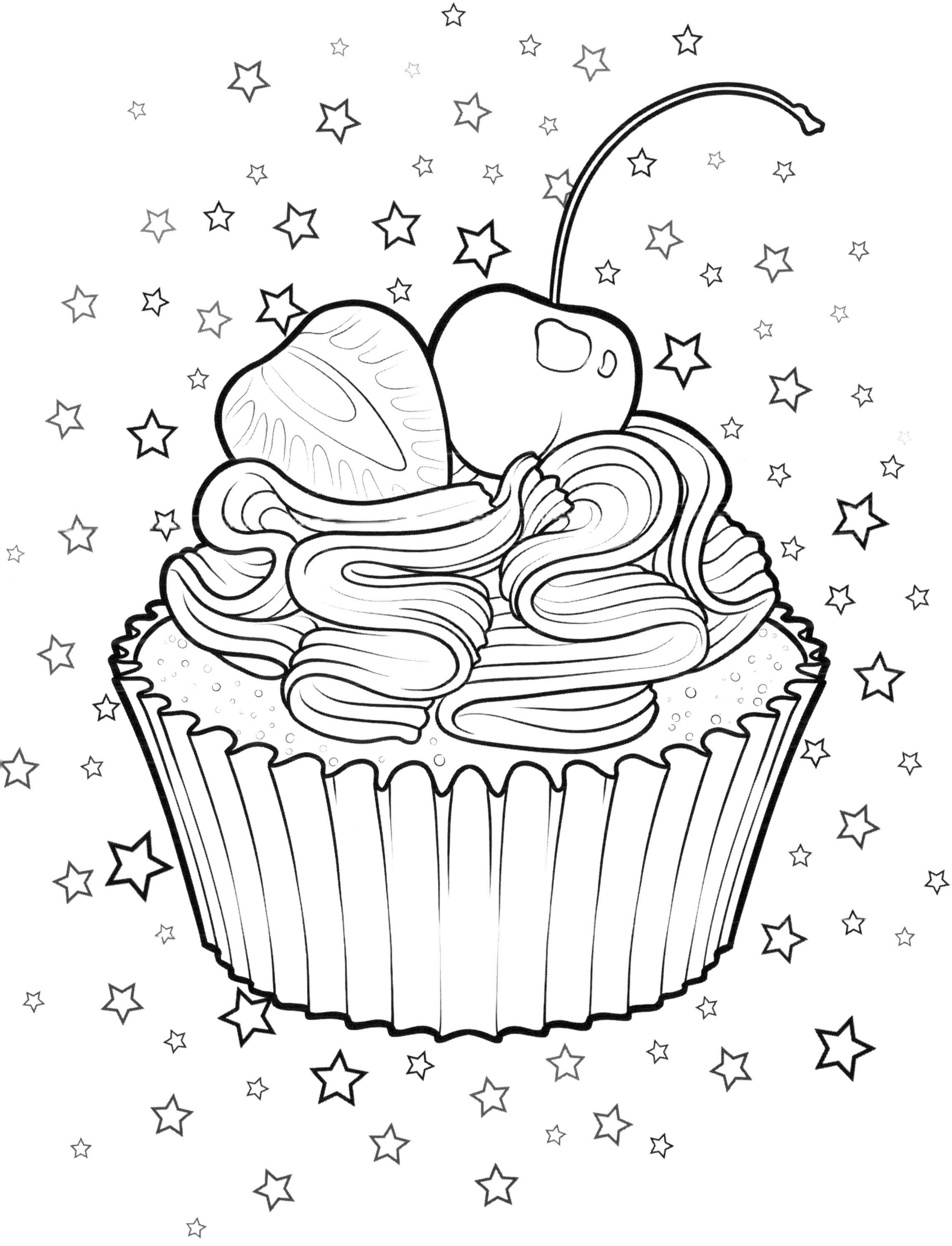

Post your work on Instagram and tag us @colormoodbooks

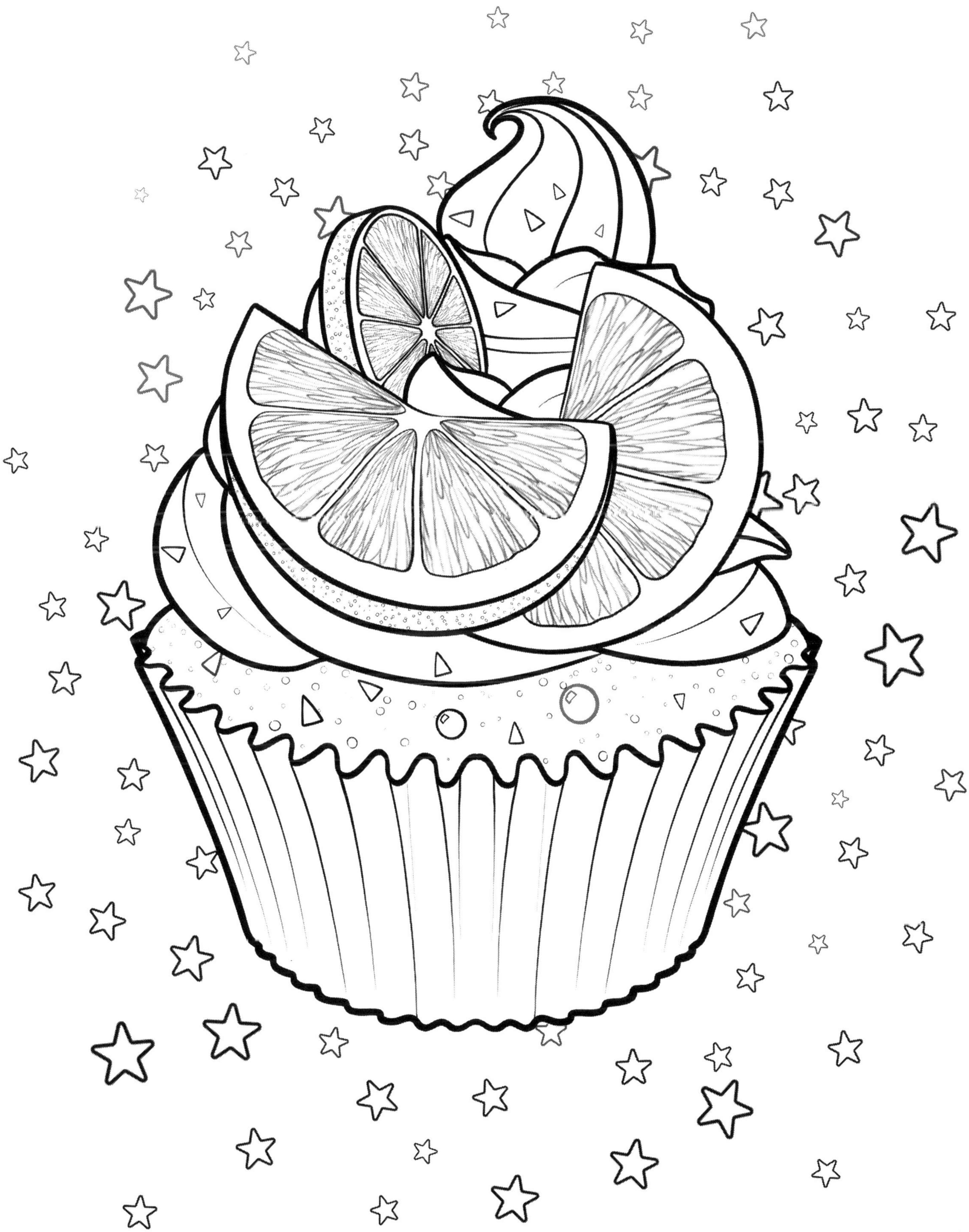

Post your work on Instagram and tag us @colormoodbooks

Post your work on Instagram and tag us @colormoodbooks

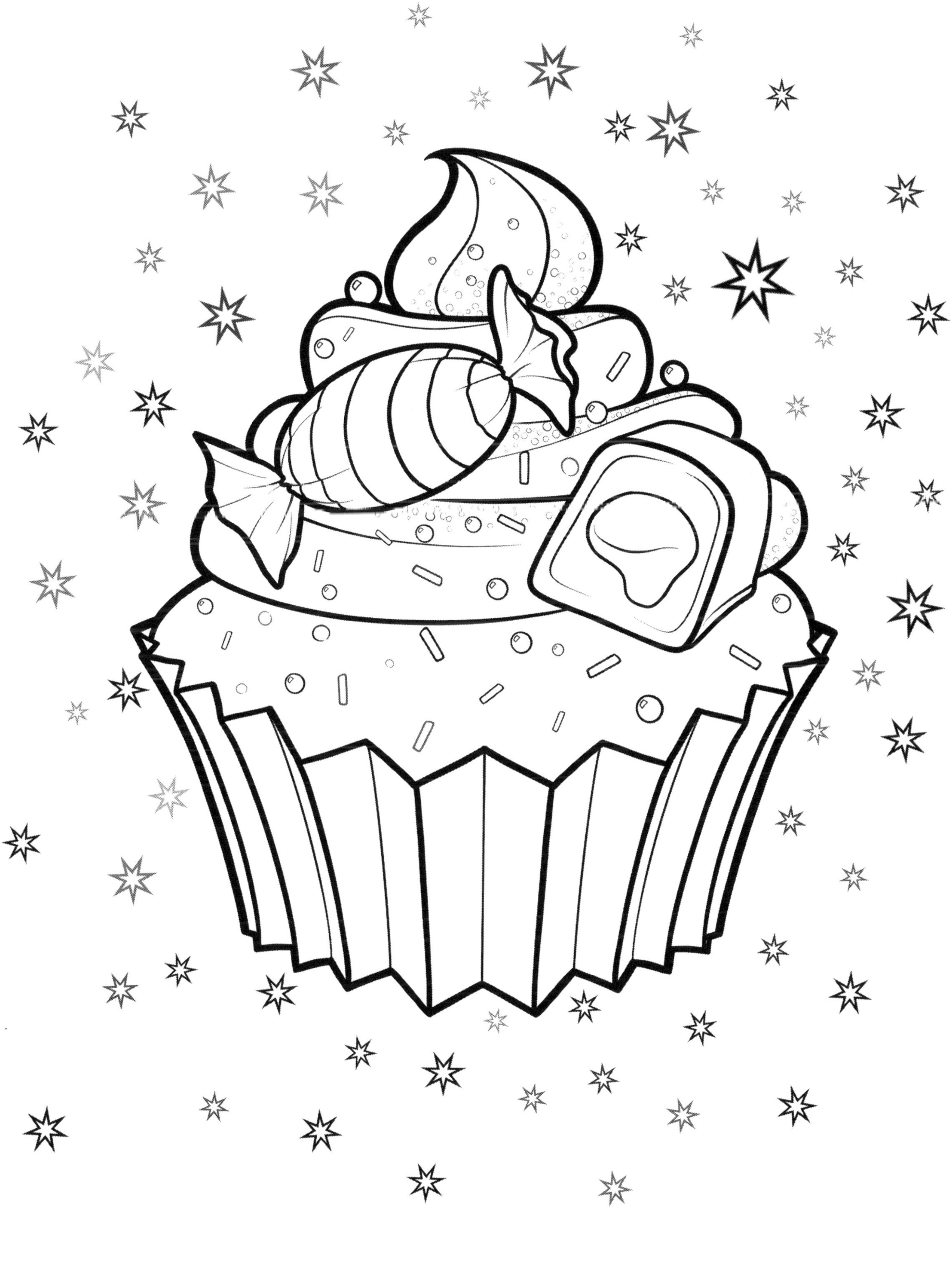

Post your work on Instagram and tag us @colormoodbooks

Post your work on Instagram and tag us @colormoodbooks

Post your work on Instagram and tag us @colormoodbooks

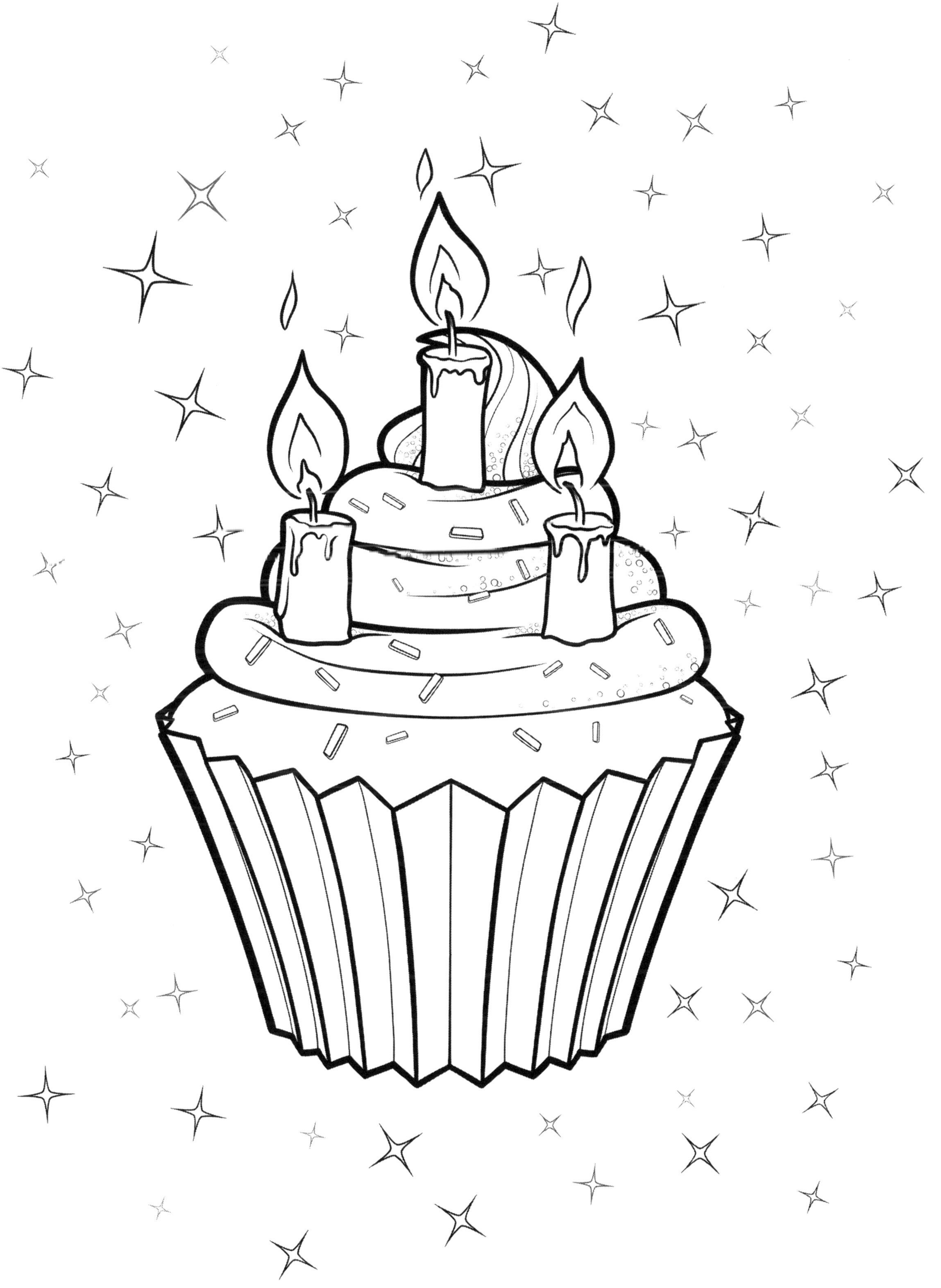

Post your work on Instagram and tag us @colormoodbooks

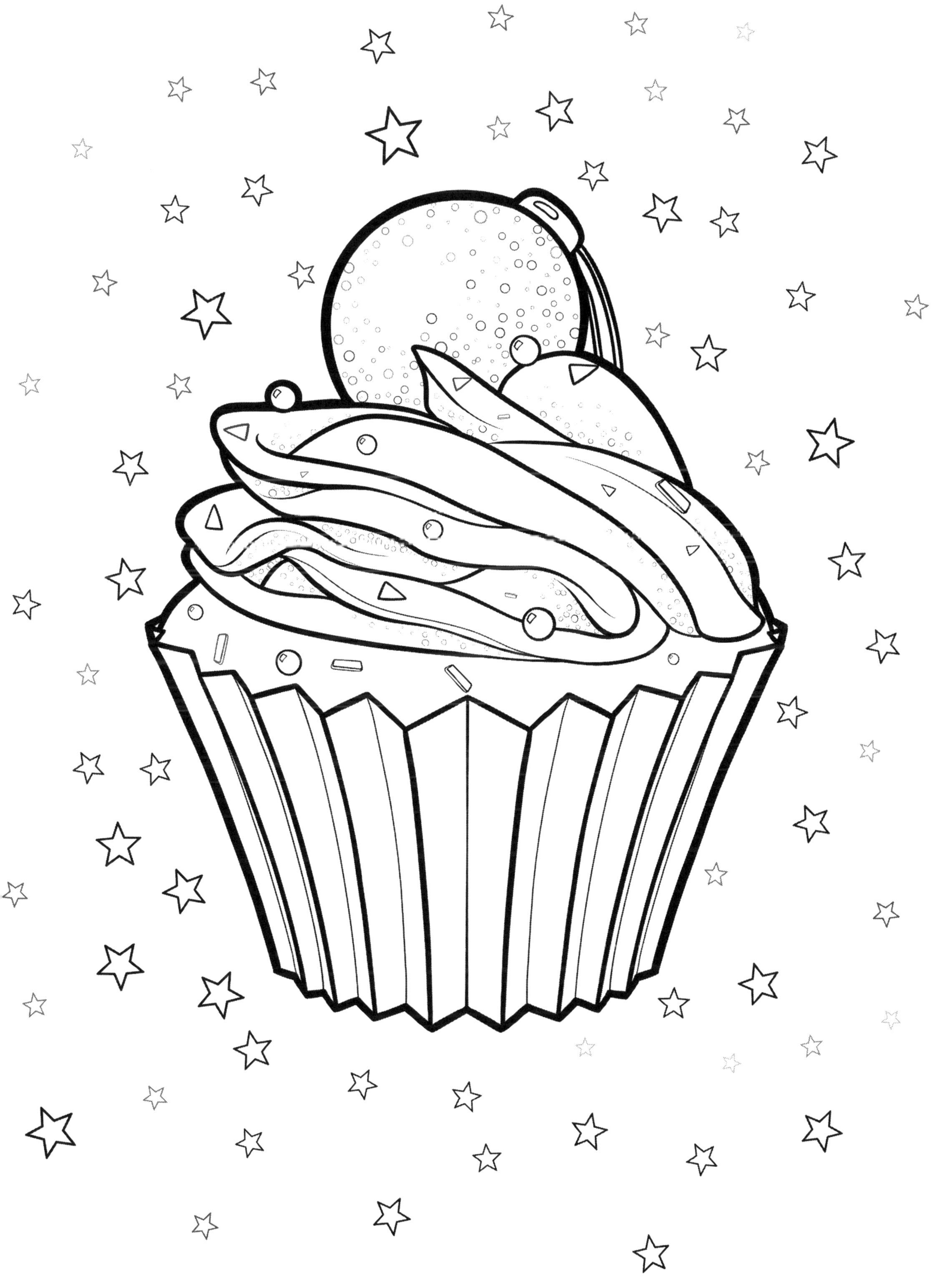

Post your work on Instagram and tag us @colormoodbooks

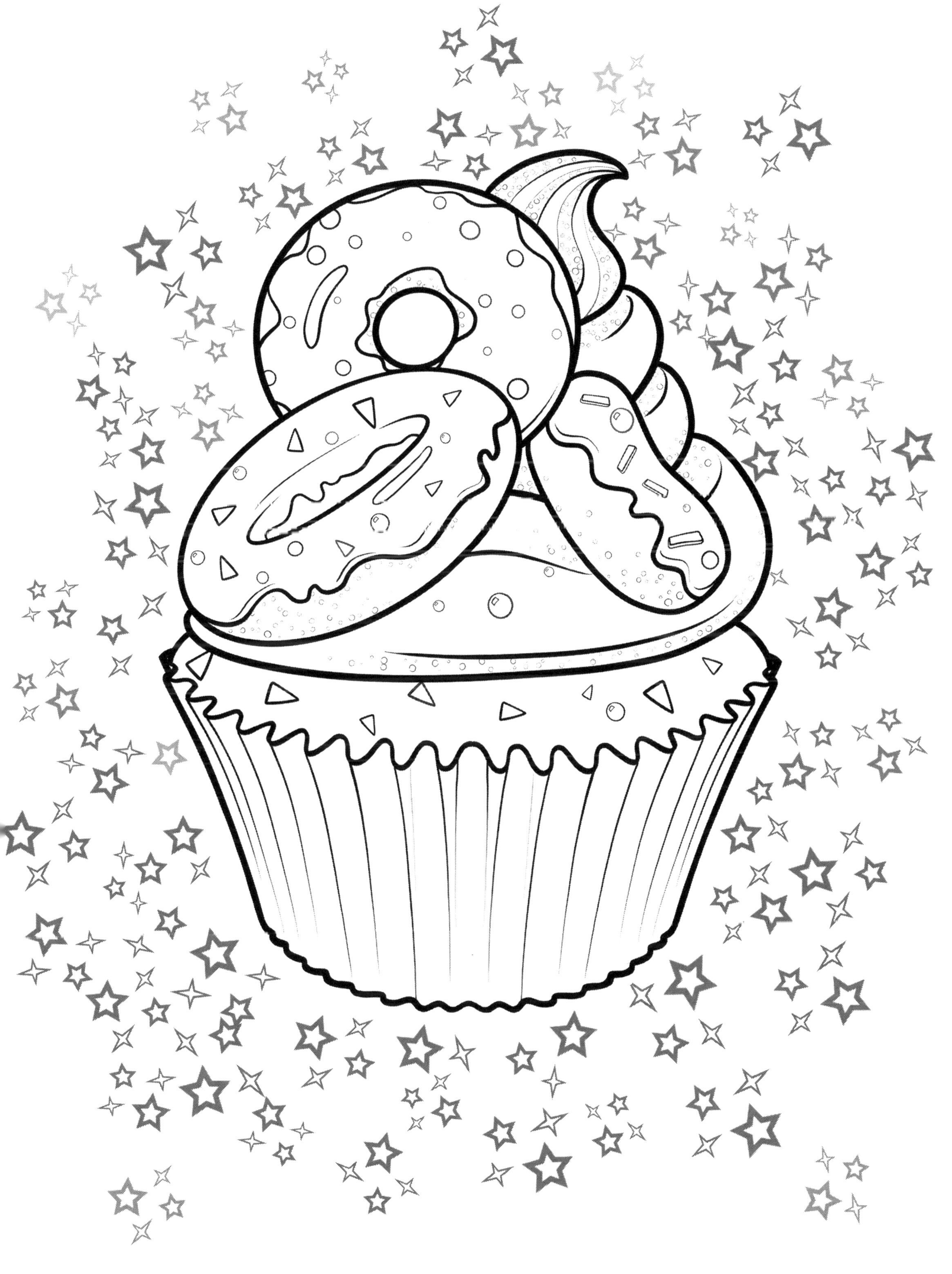

Post your work on Instagram and tag us @colormoodbooks

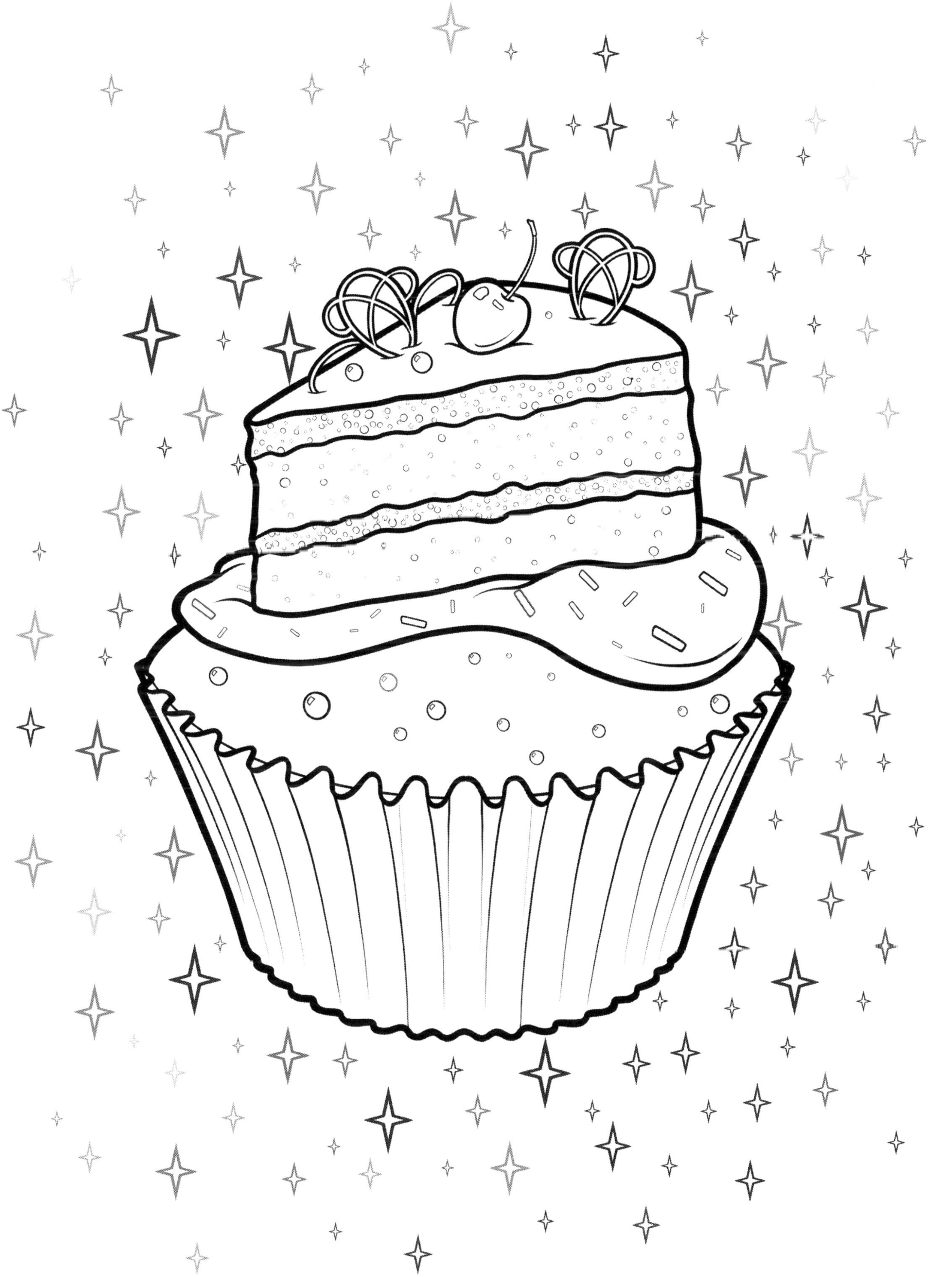

Post your work on Instagram and tag us @colormoodbooks

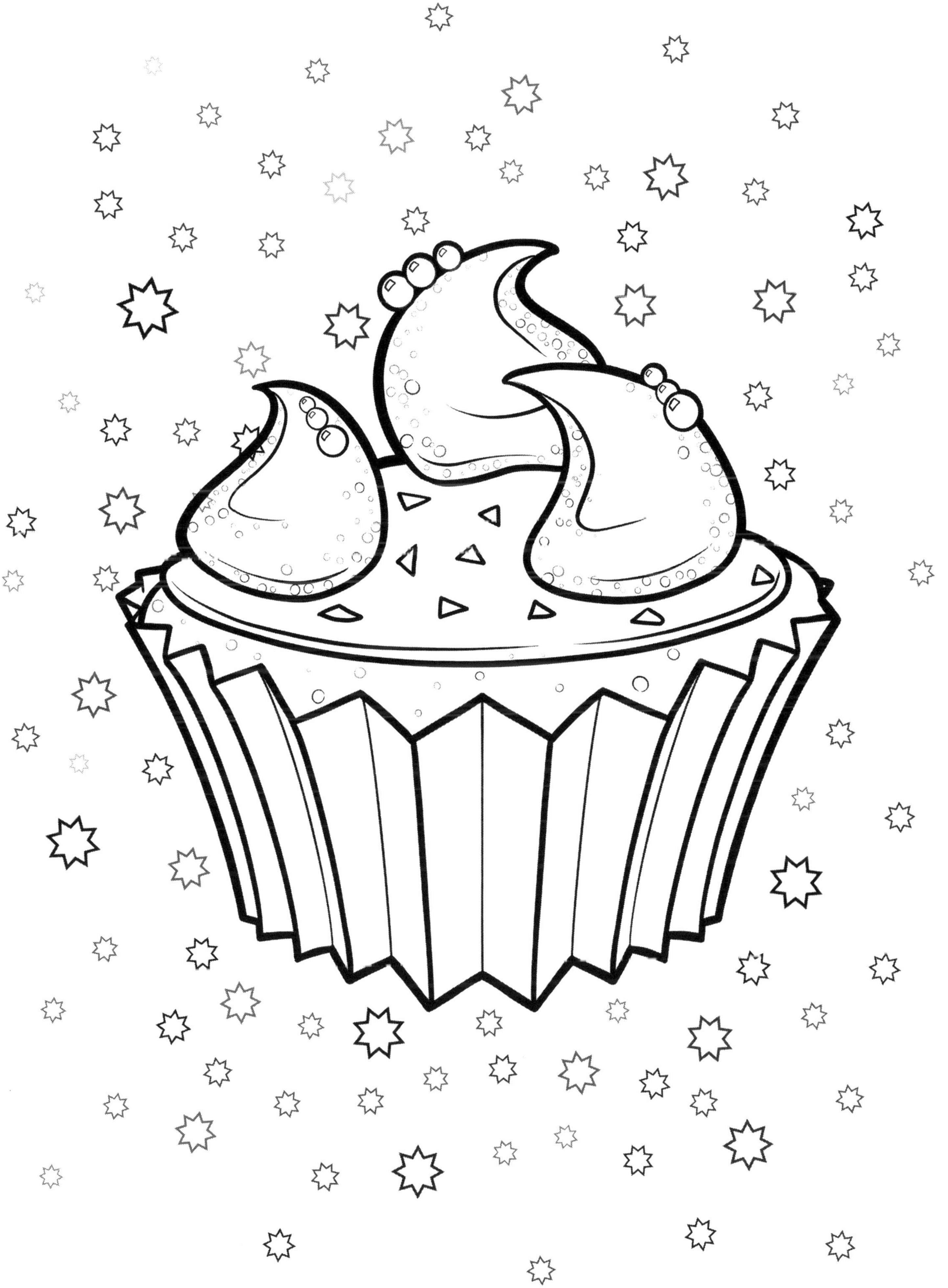

Post your work on Instagram and tag us @colormoodbooks

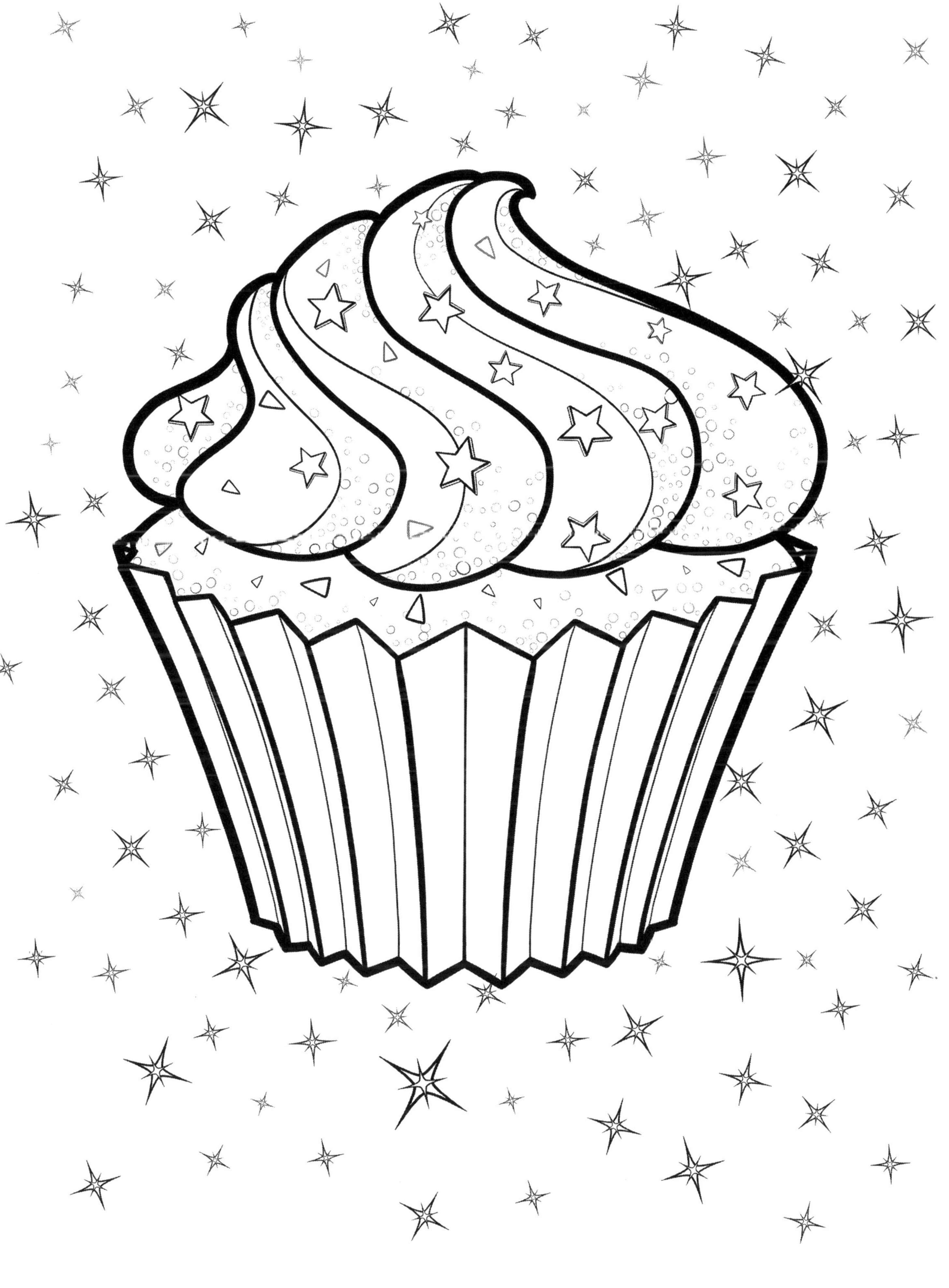

Post your work on Instagram and tag us @colormoodbooks

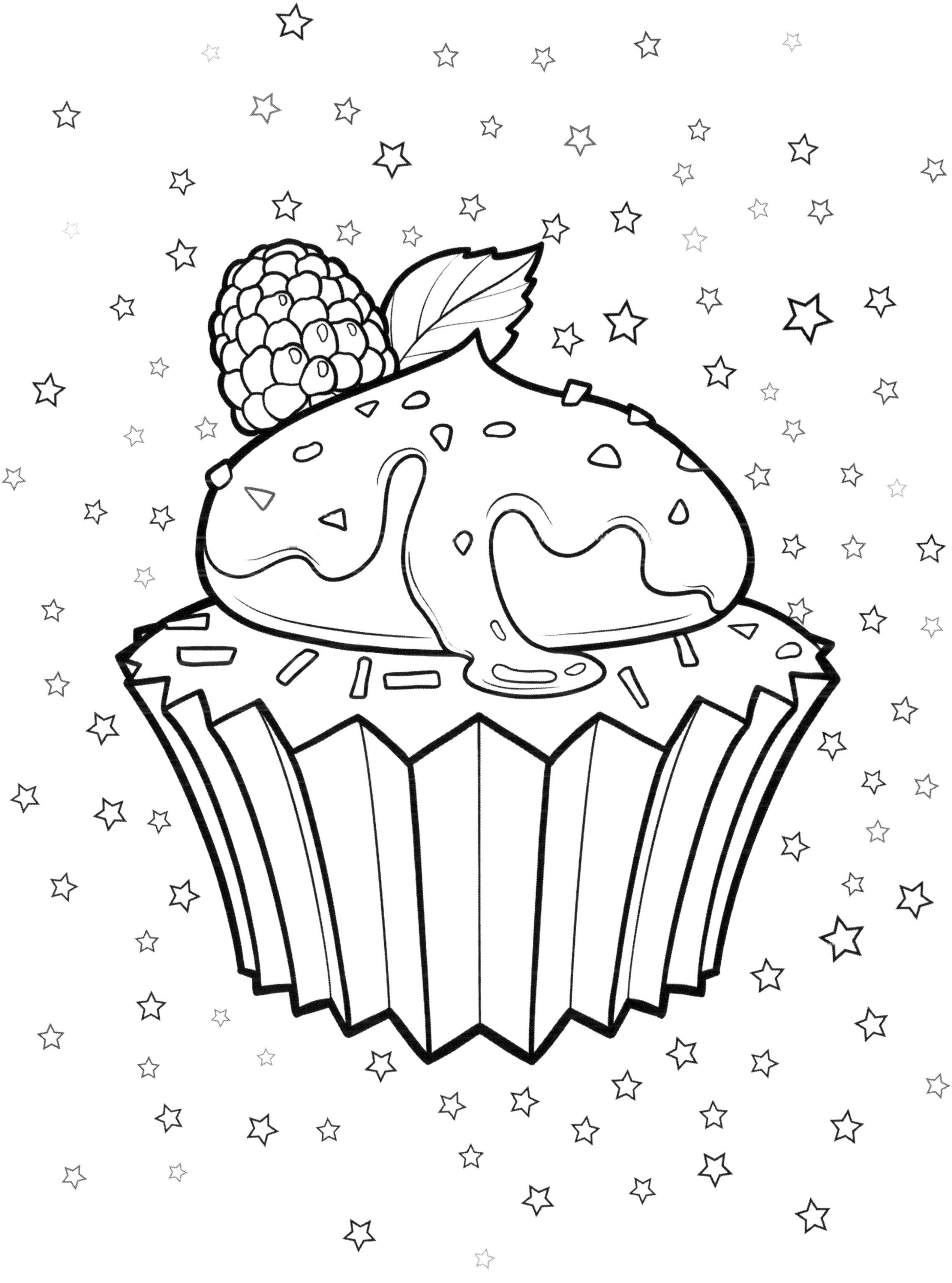

Post your work on Instagram and tag us @colormoodbooks

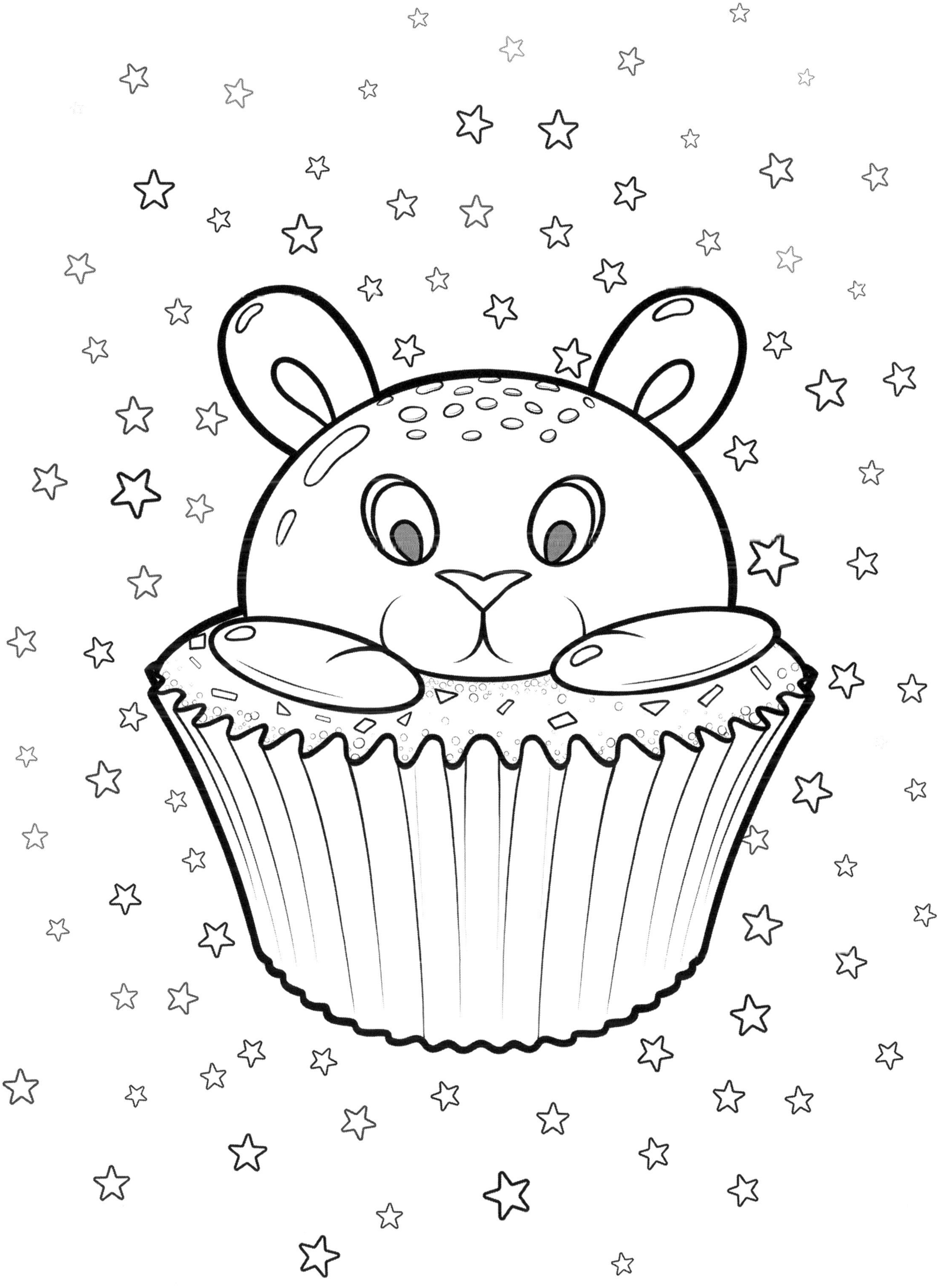

Post your work on Instagram and tag us @colormoodbooks

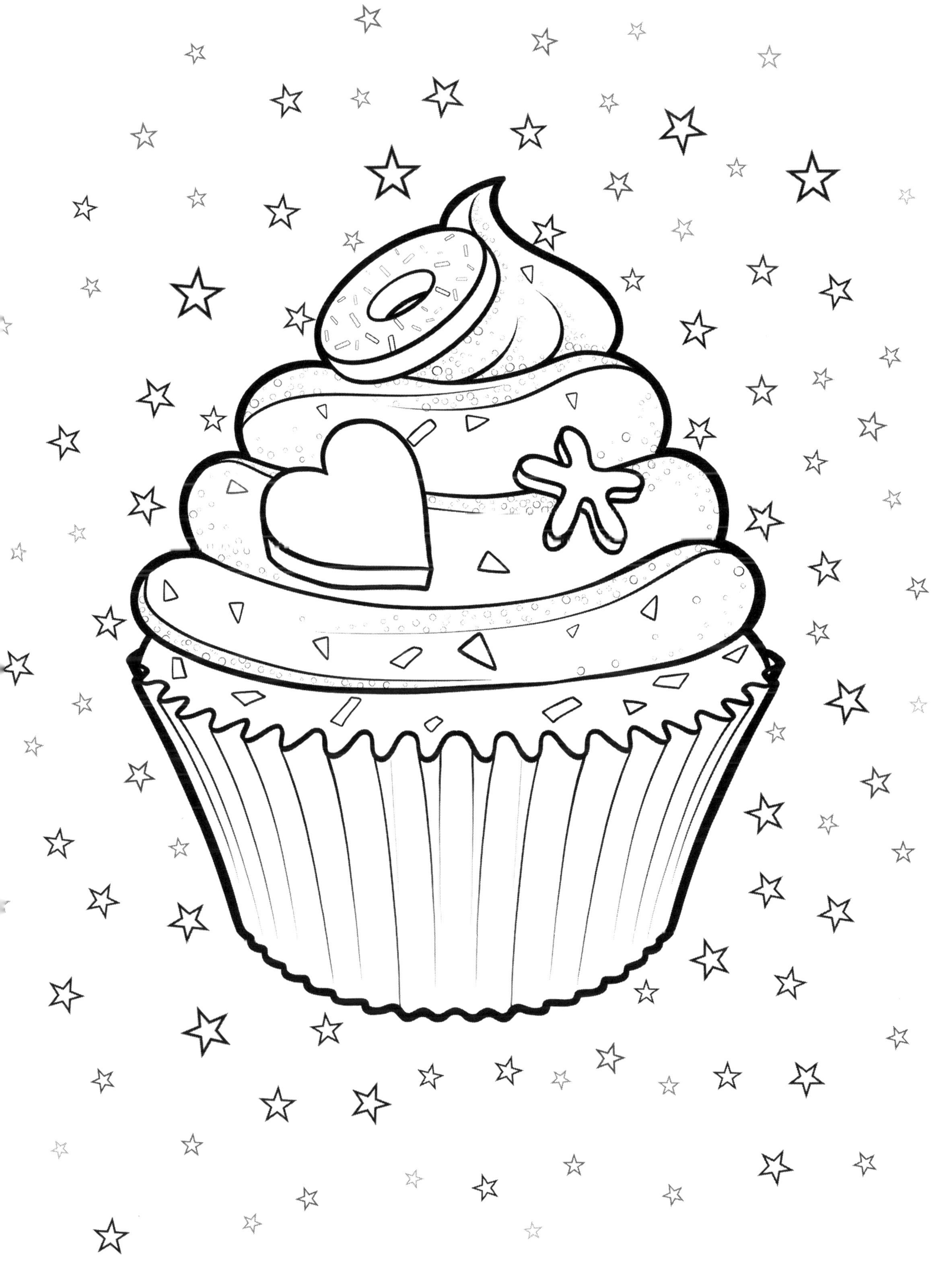

Post your work on Instagram and tag us @colormoodbooks

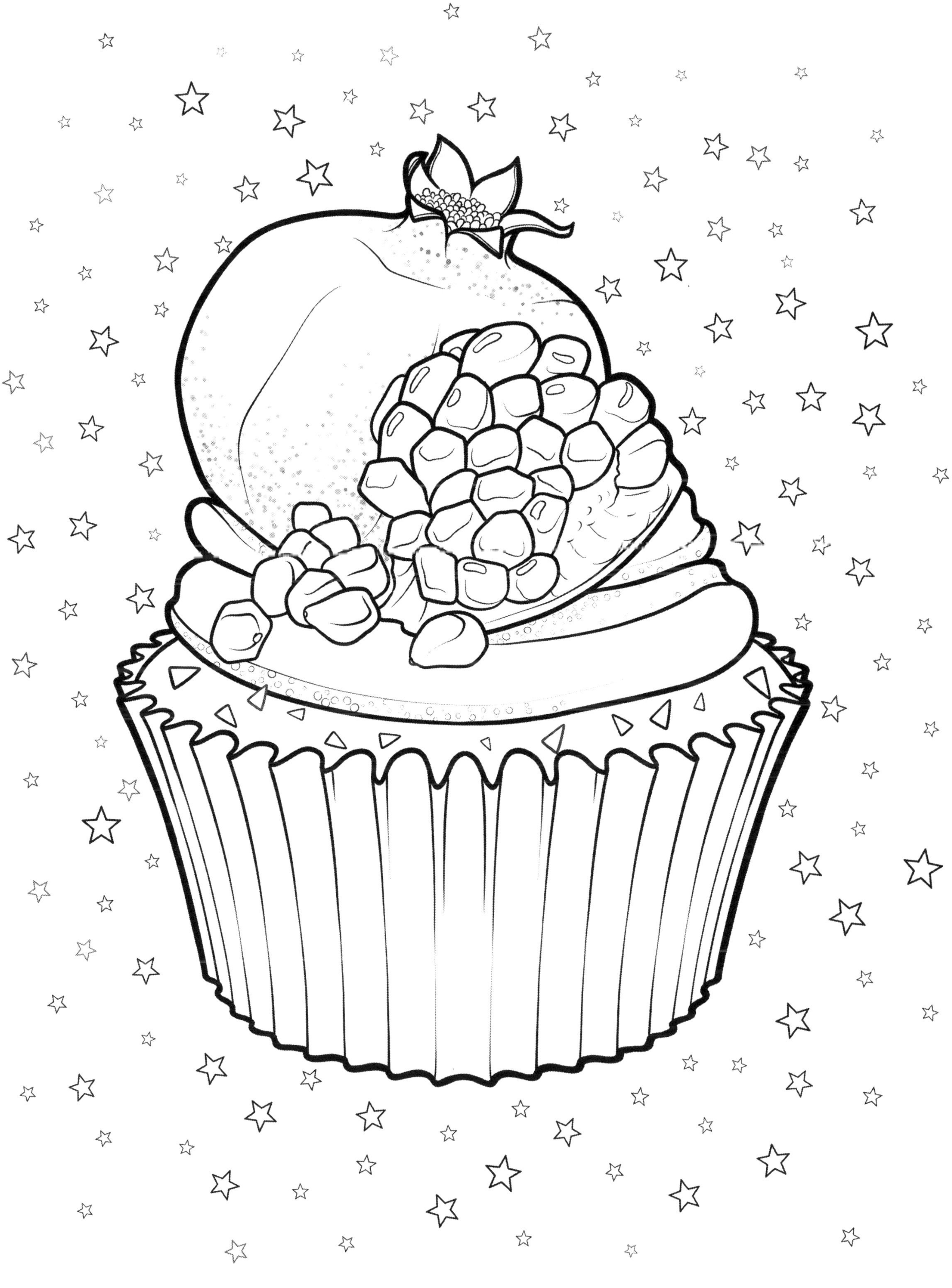

Post your work on Instagram and tag us @colormoodbooks

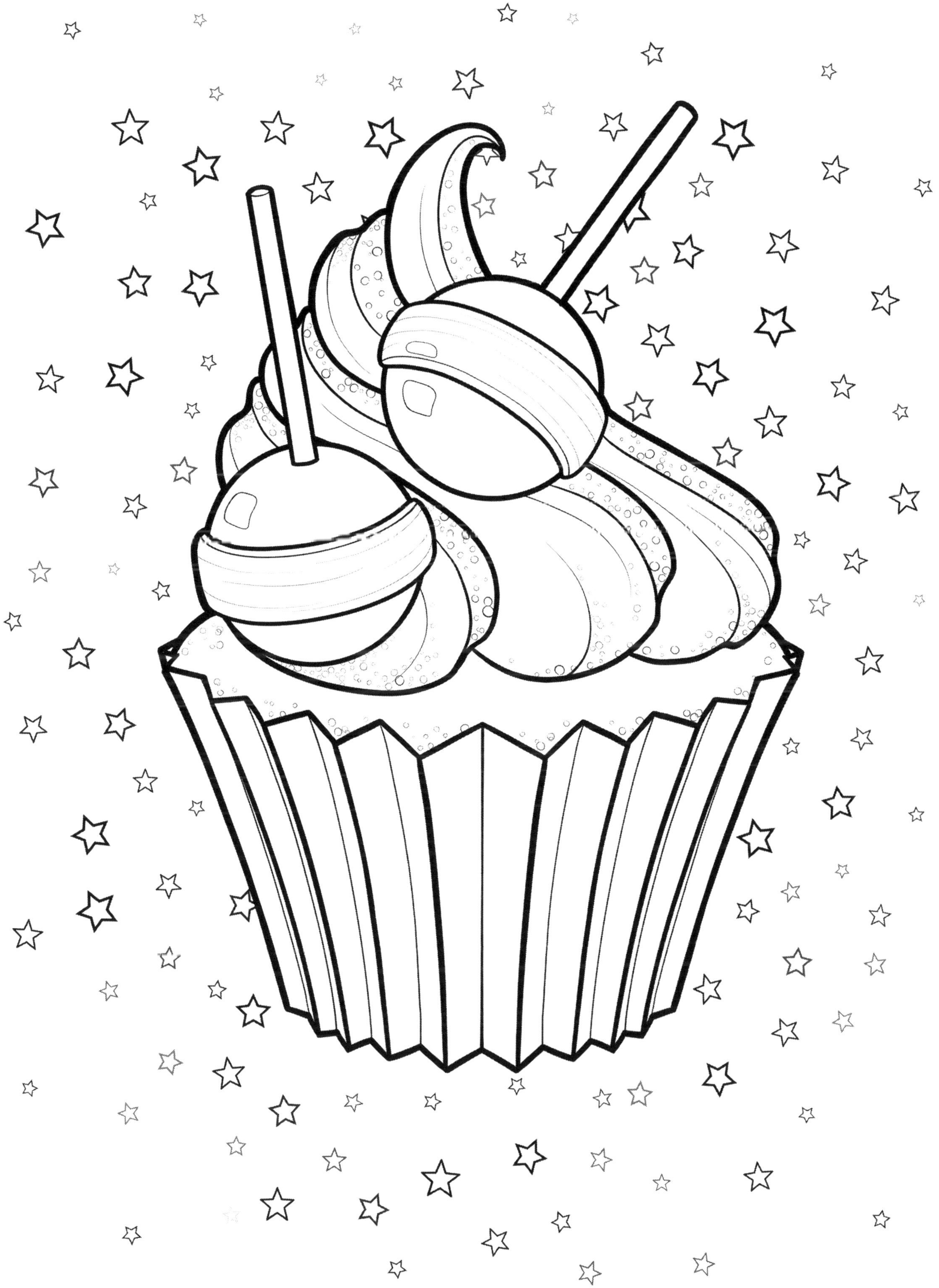

Post your work on Instagram and tag us @colormoodbooks

Post your work on Instagram and tag us @colormoodbooks

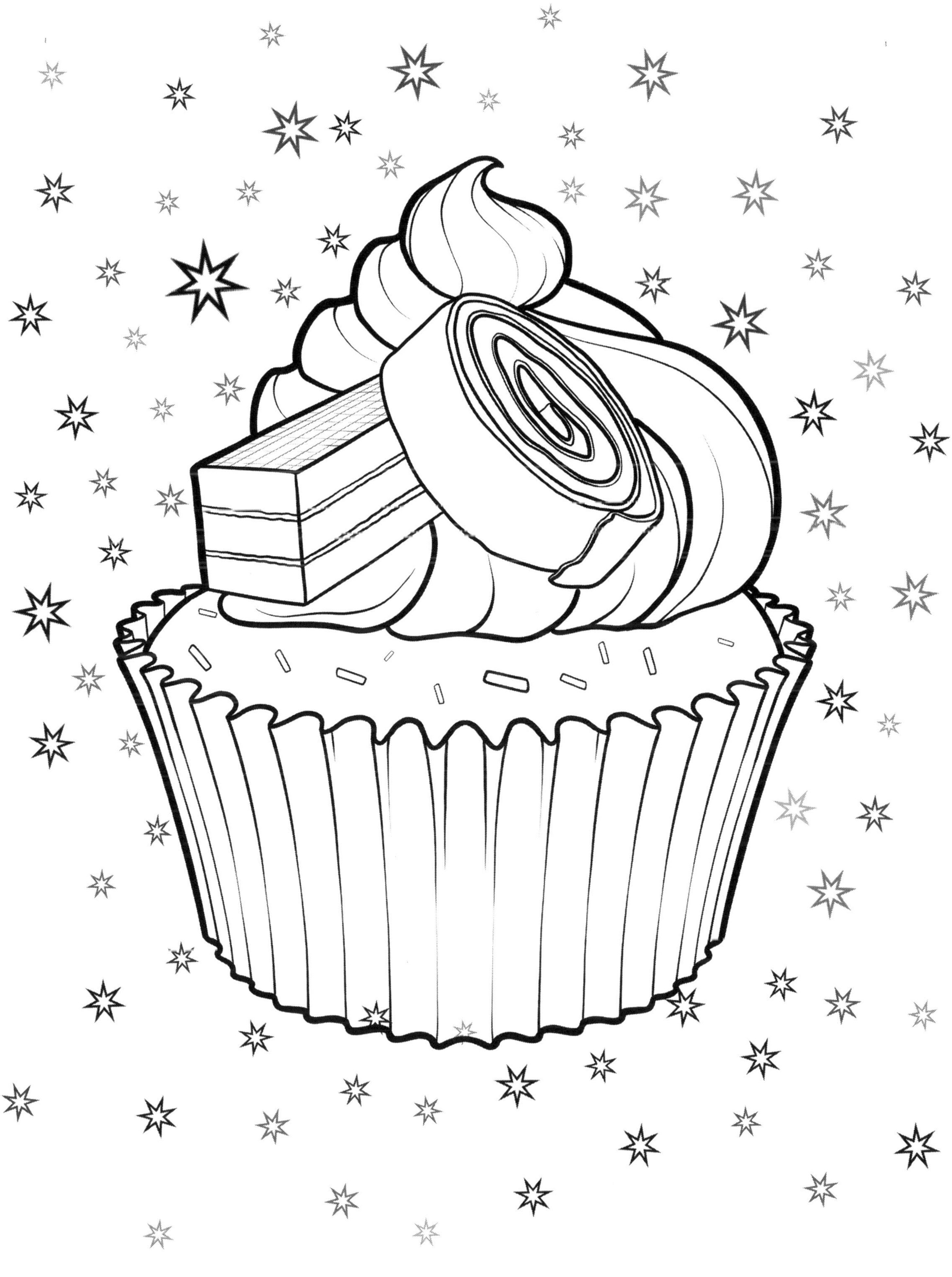

Post your work on Instagram and tag us @colormoodbooks

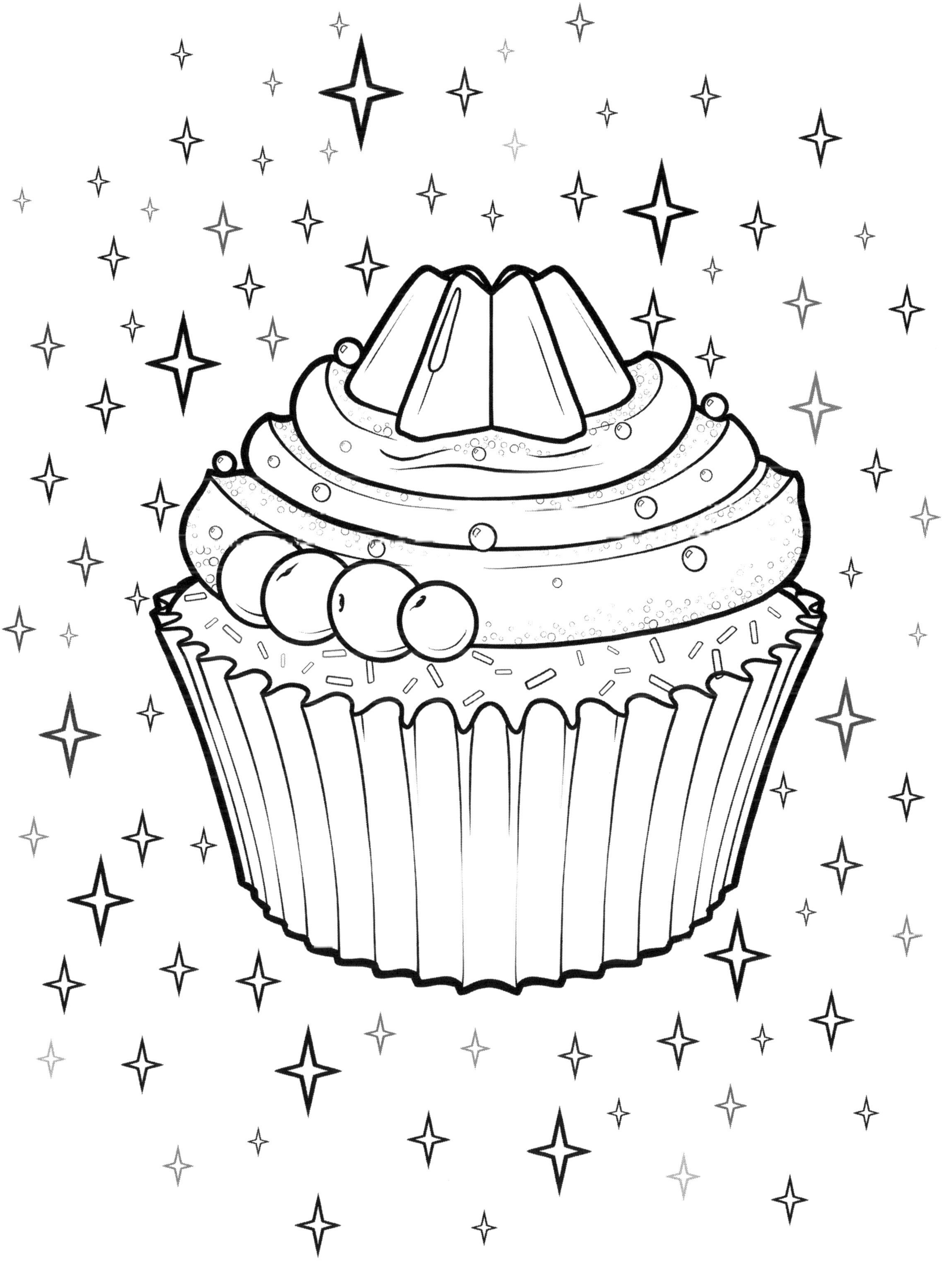

Post your work on Instagram and tag us @colormoodbooks

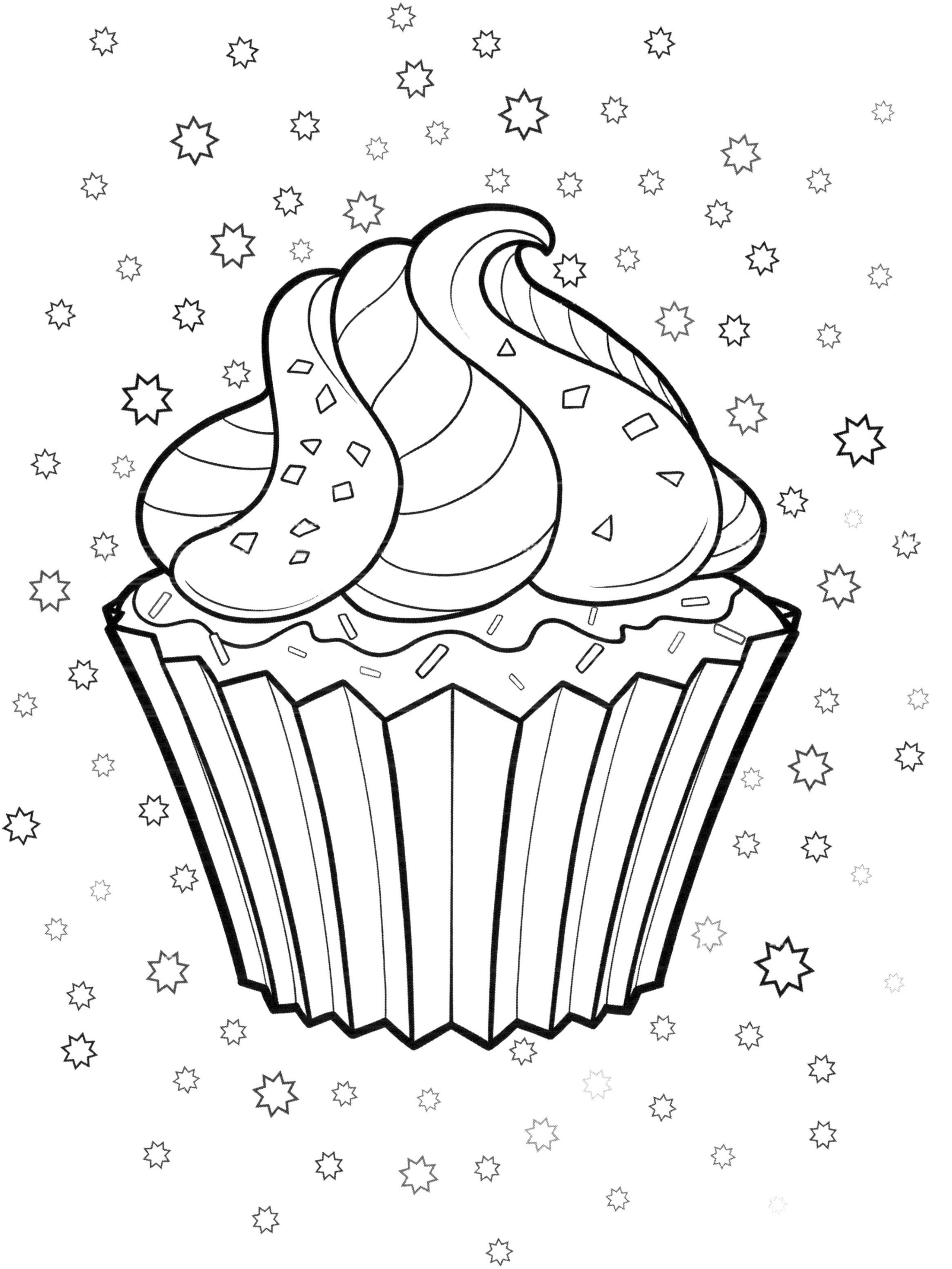

Post your work on Instagram and tag us @colormoodbooks

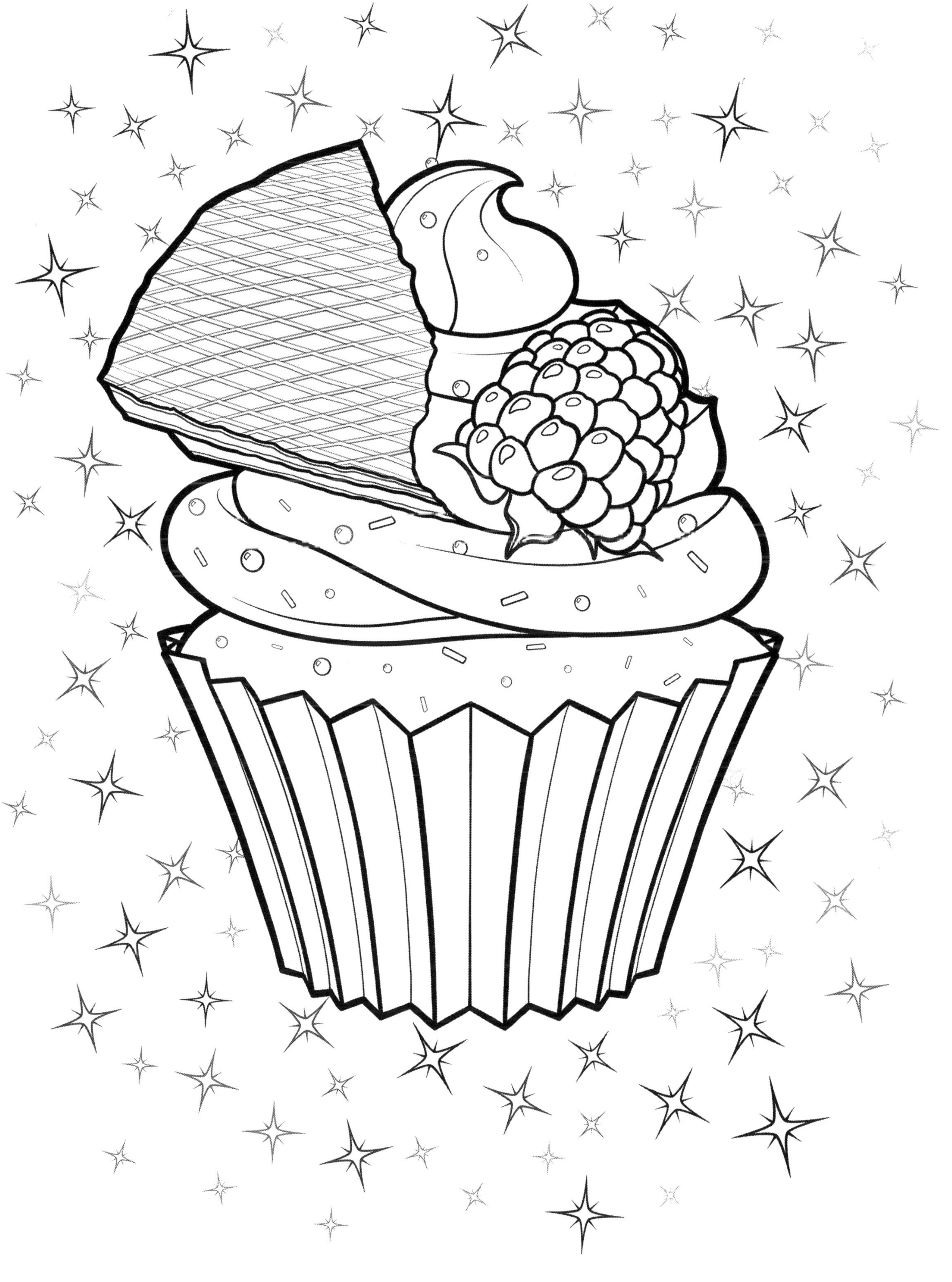

Post your work on Instagram and tag us @colormoodbooks

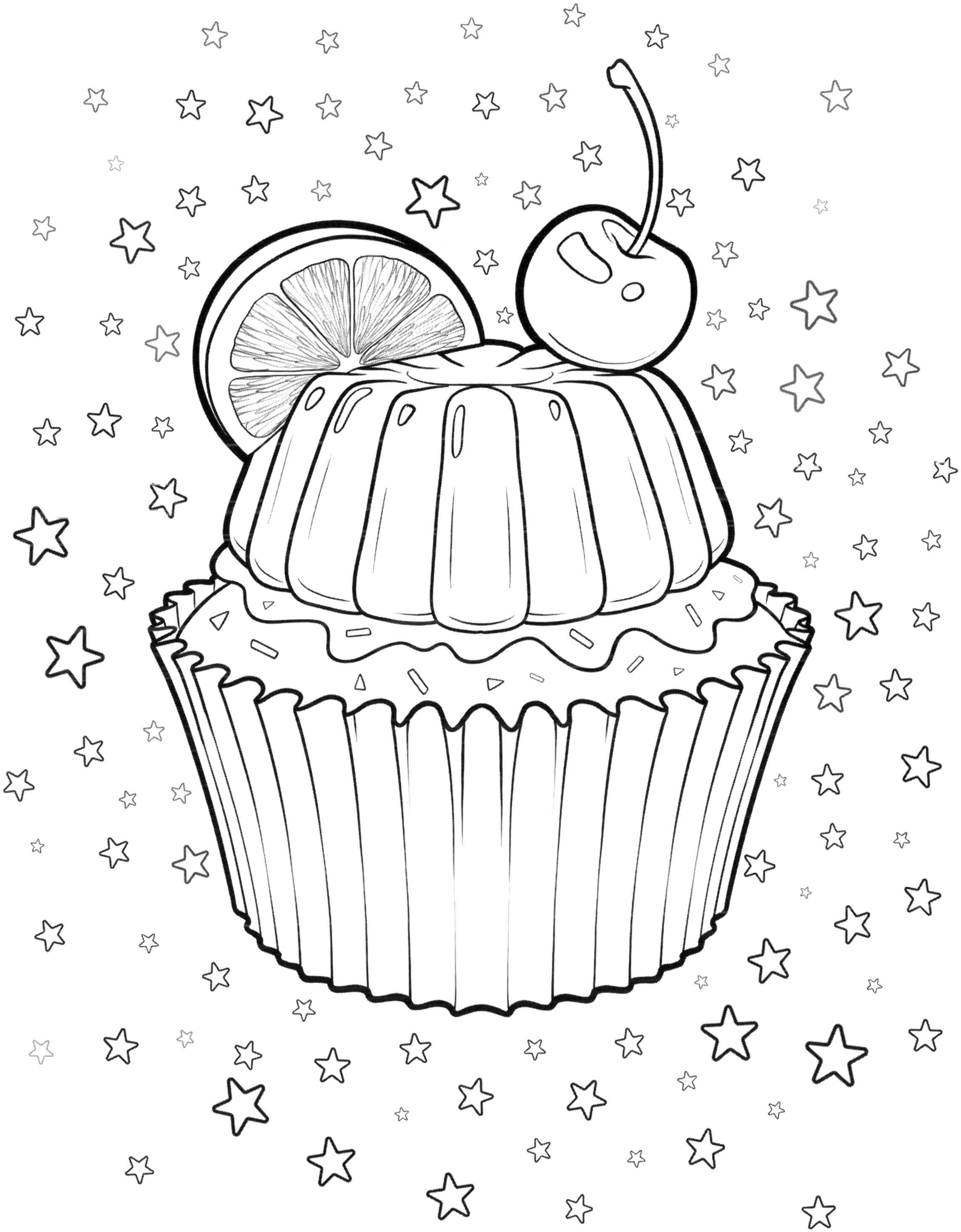

Post your work on Instagram and tag us @colormoodbooks

Post your work on Instagram and tag us @colormoodbooks

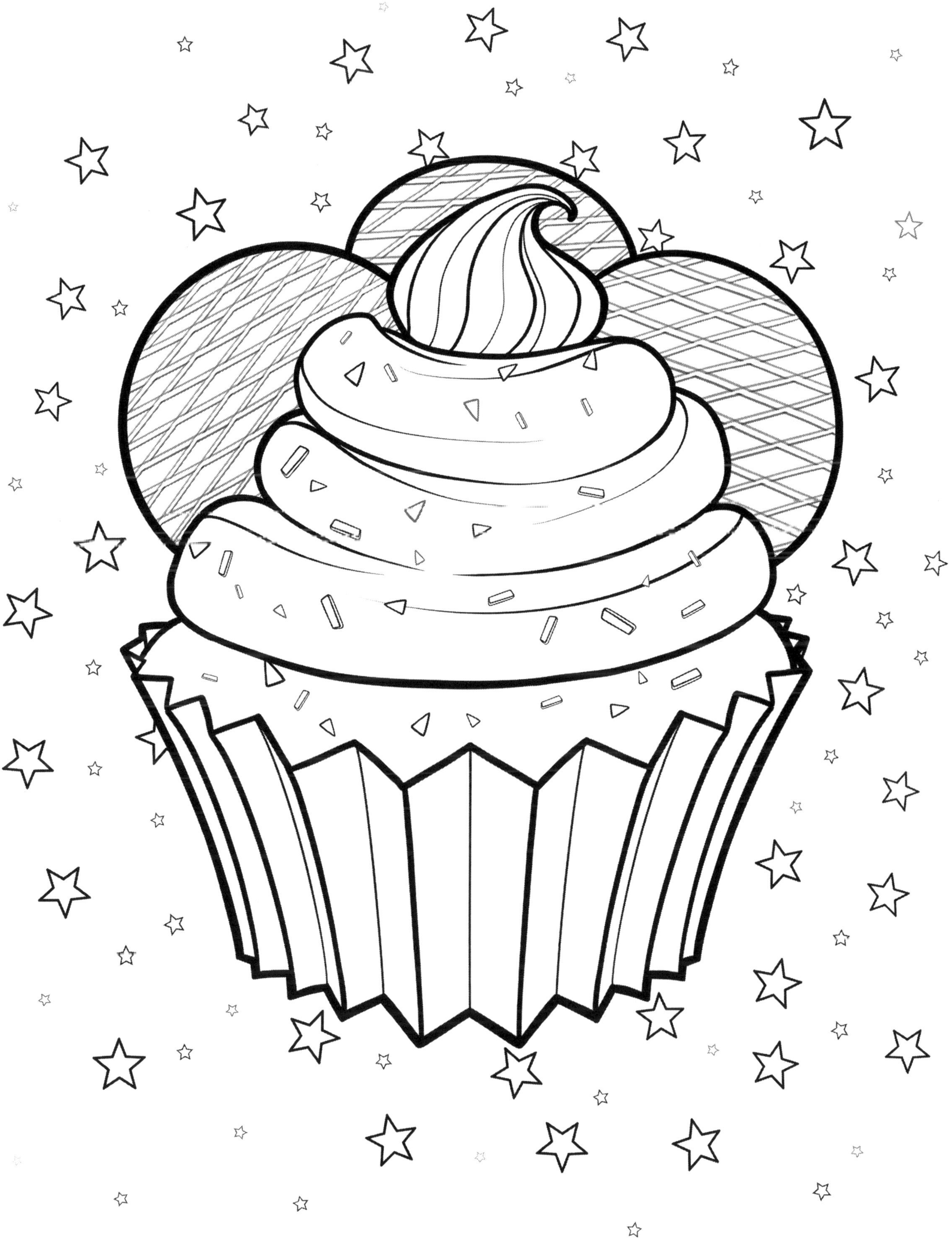

Post your work on Instagram and tag us @colormoodbooks

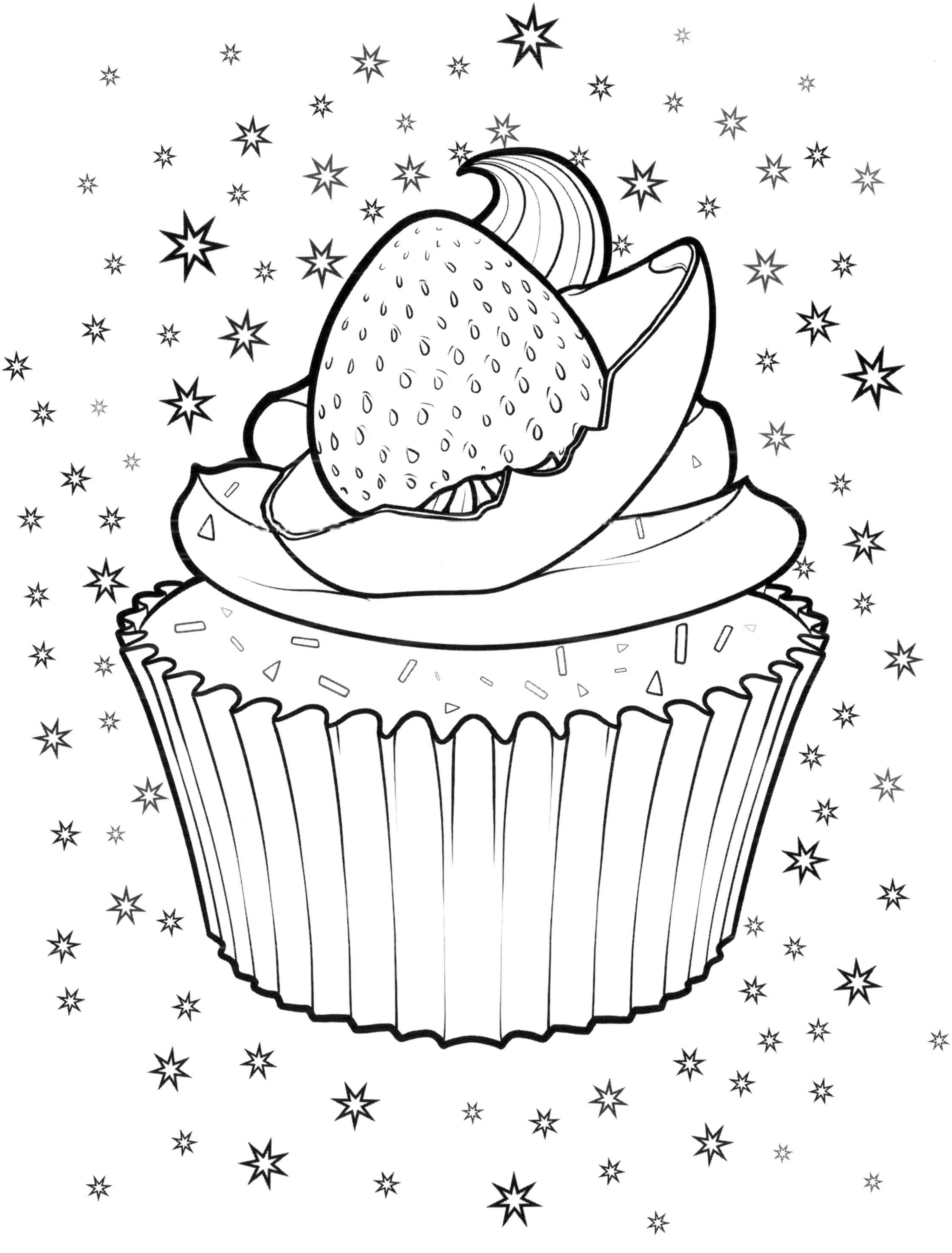

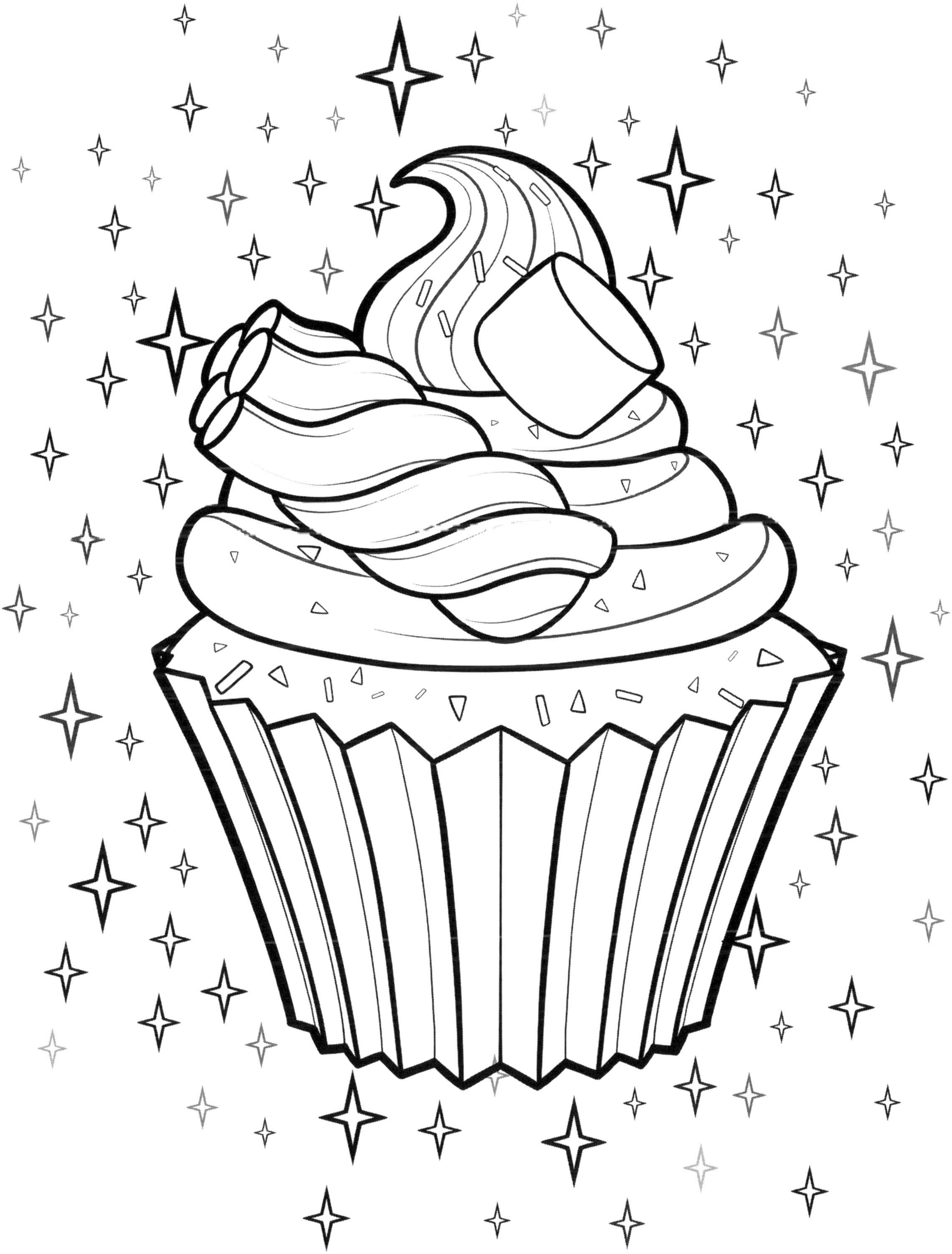

Post your work on Instagram and tag us @colormoodbooks

Sweet

Post your work on Instagram and tag us @colormoodbooks

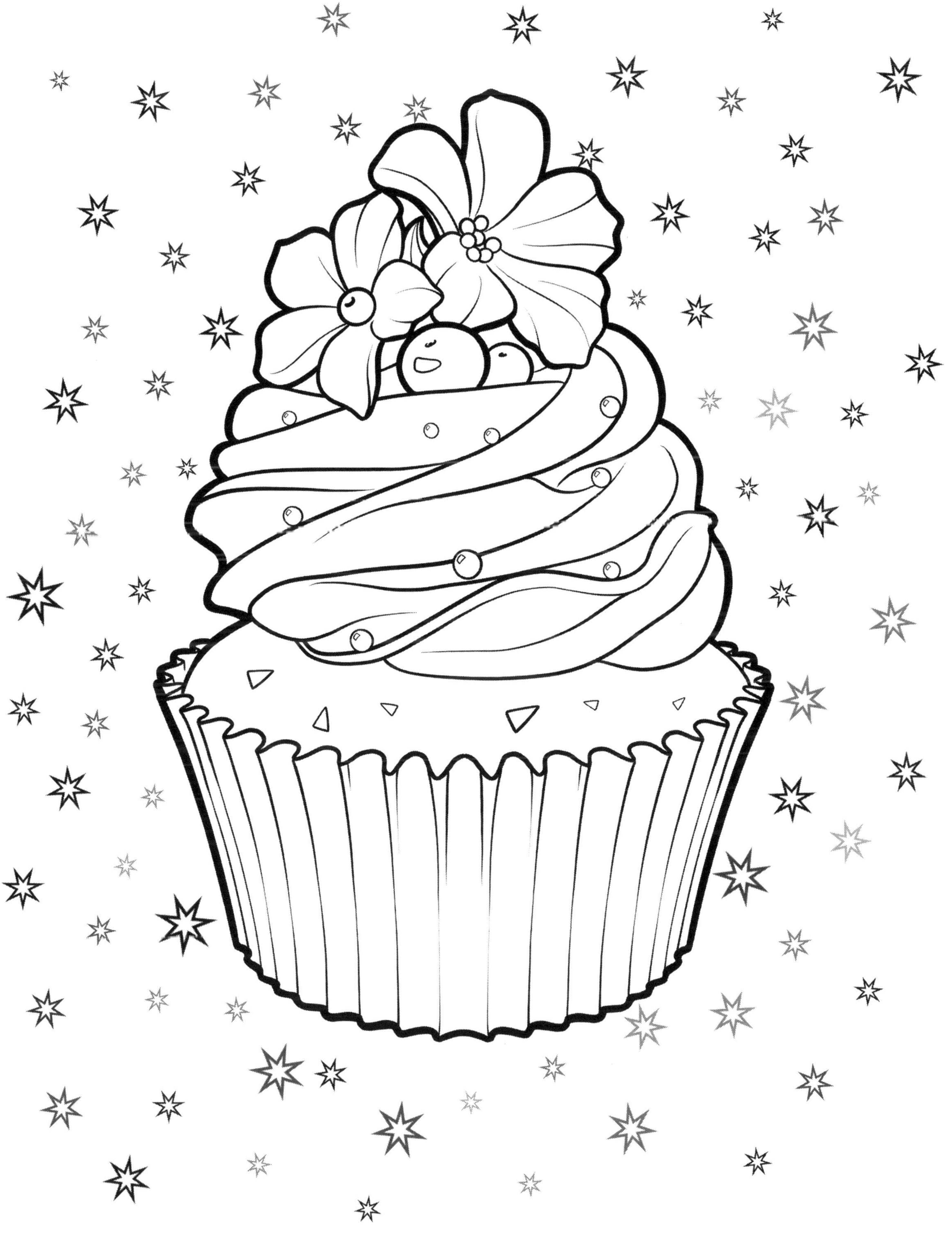

Post your work on Instagram and tag us @colormoodbooks

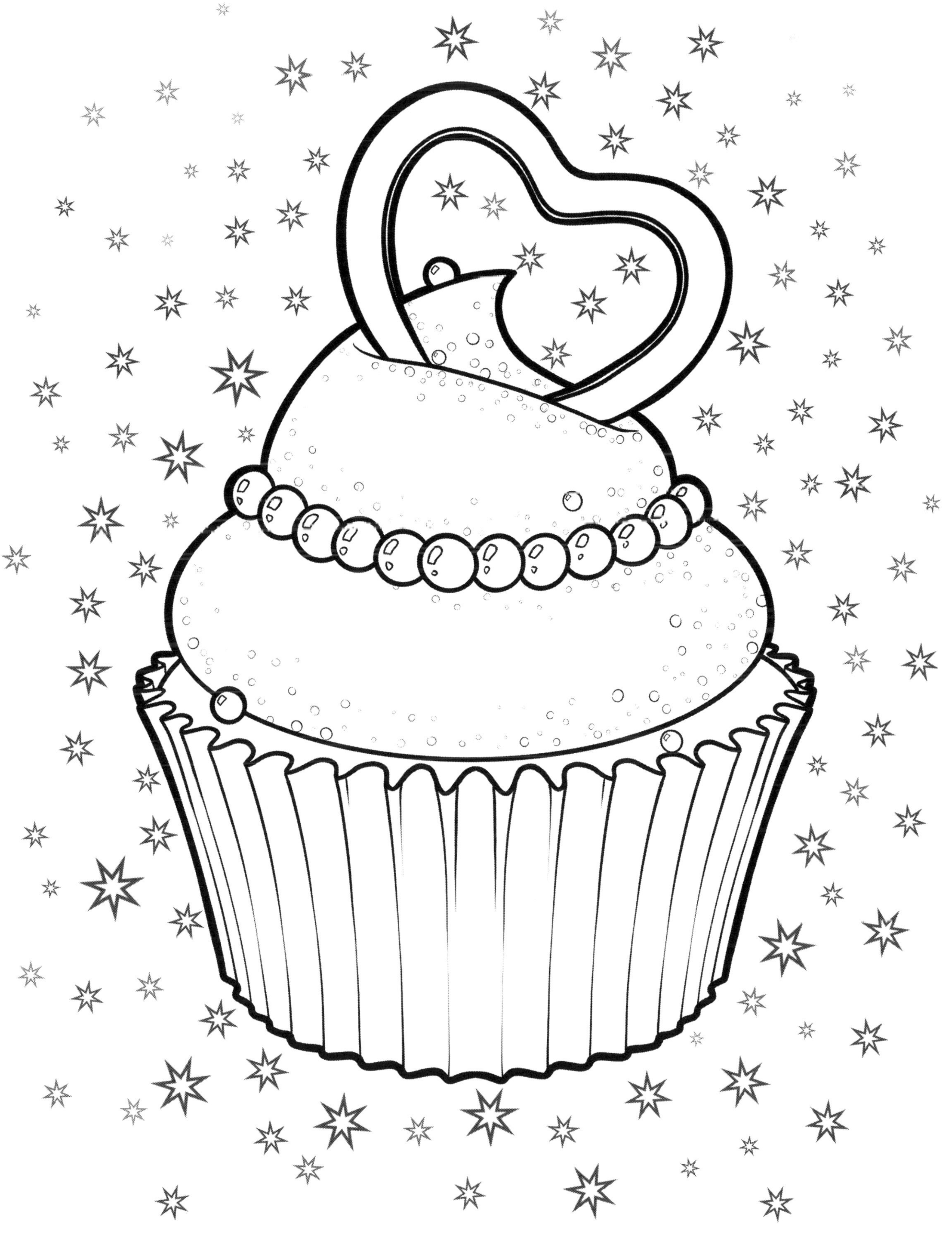

Post your work on Instagram and tag us @colormoodbooks

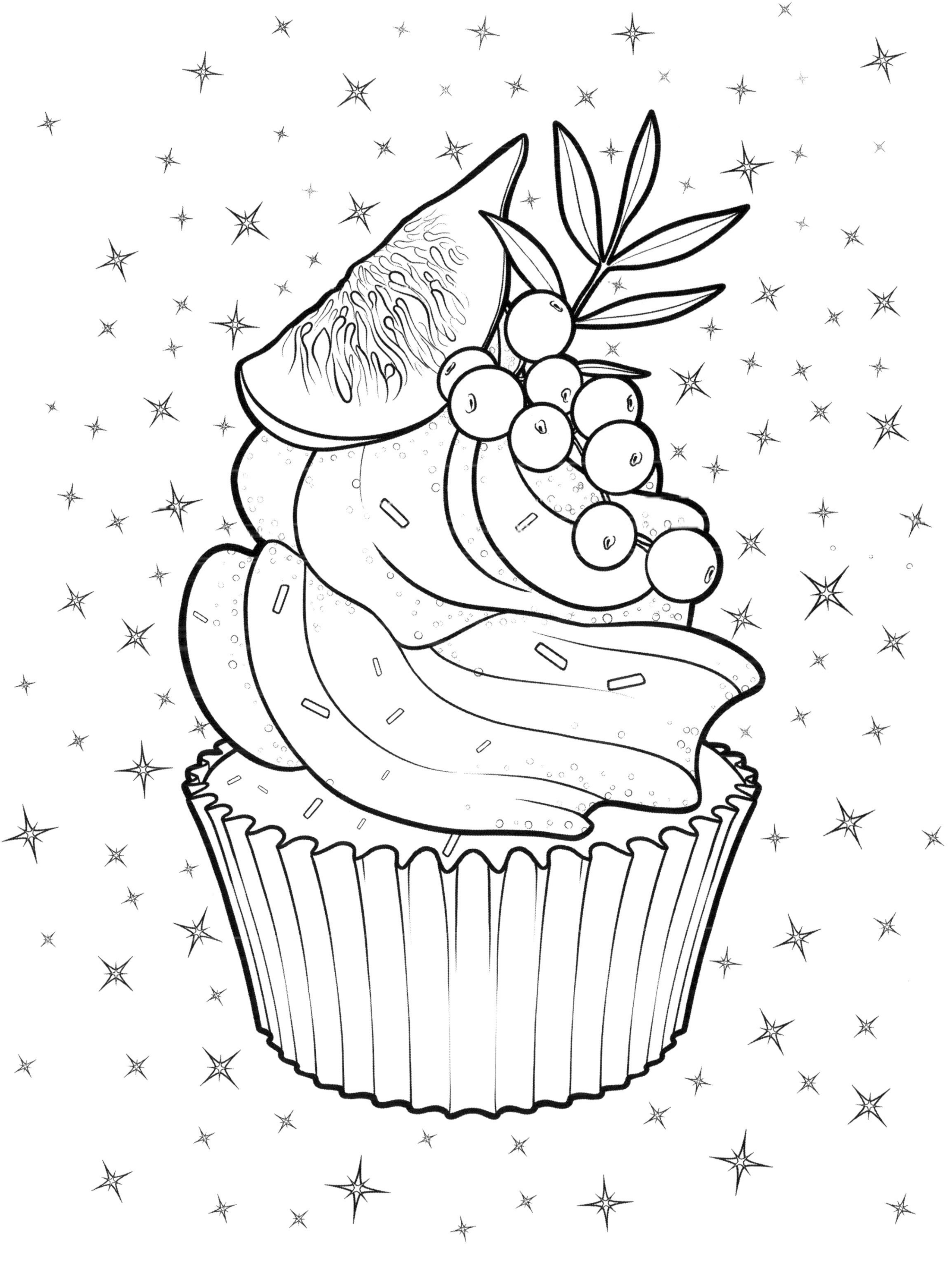

Post your work on Instagram and tag us @colormoodbooks

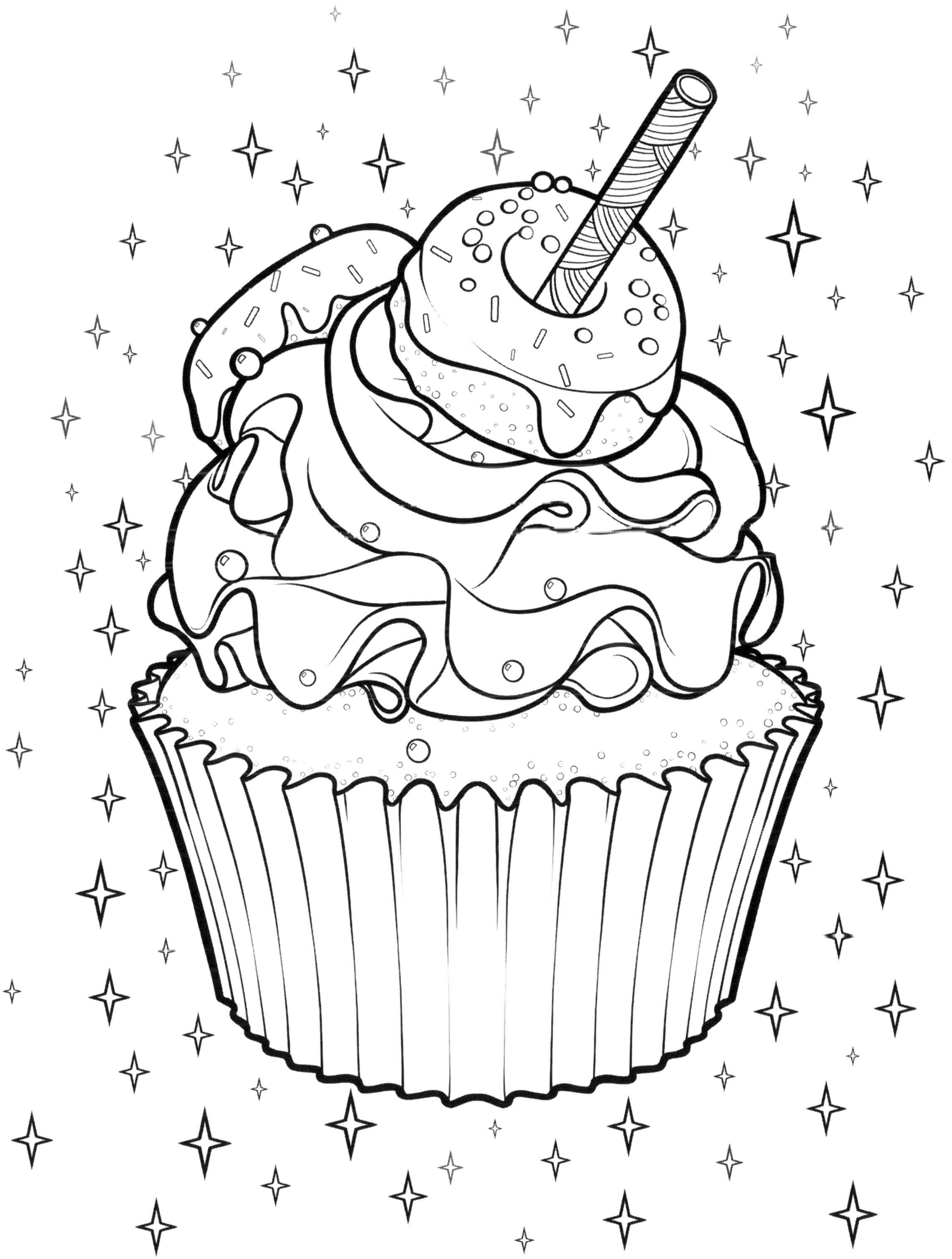

Post your work on Instagram and tag us @colormoodbooks

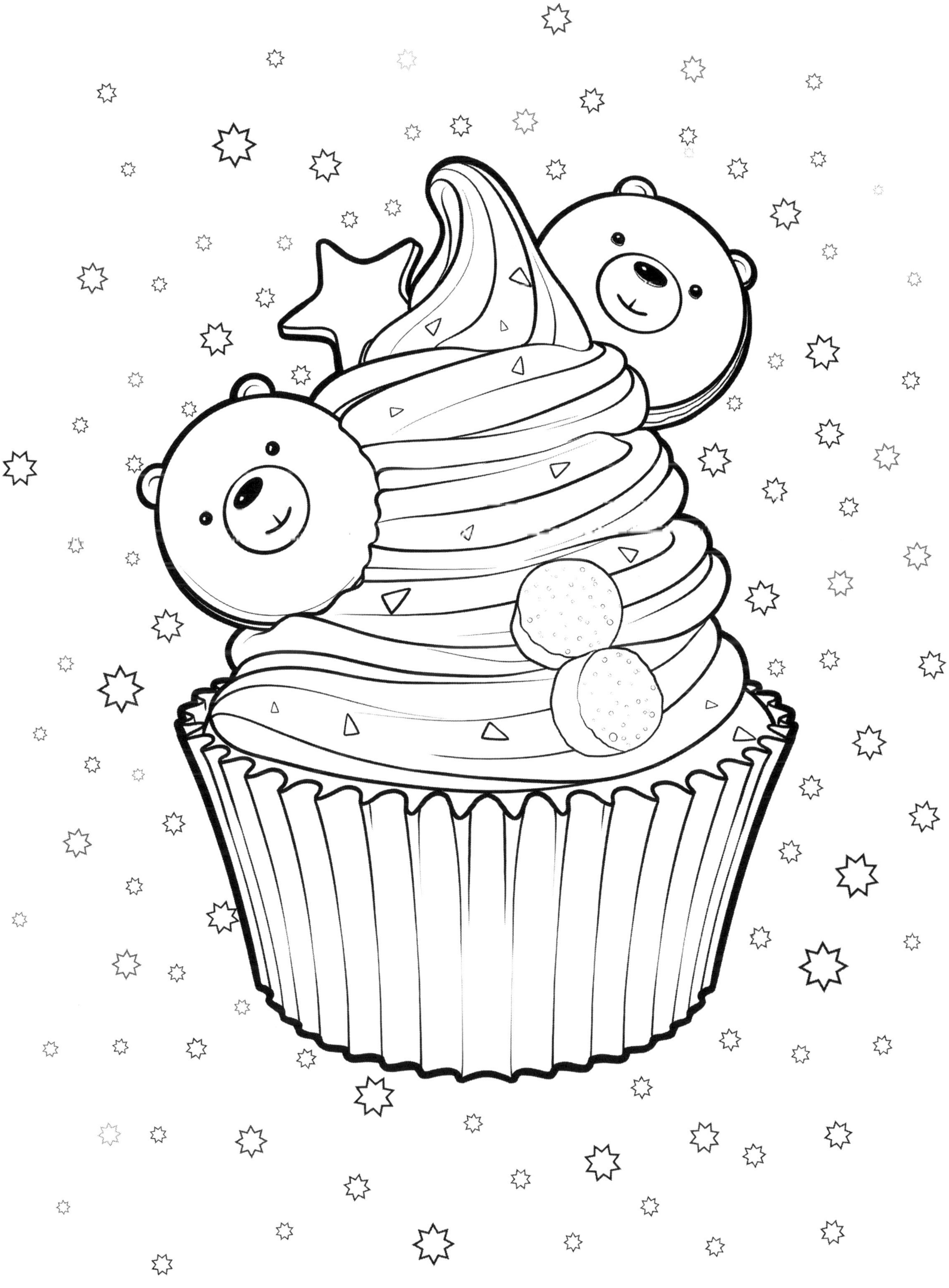

Post your work on Instagram and tag us @colormoodbooks

HAPPY

COLORMOOD
BOOKS®

Thank you for your purchase!

If you've had a pleasant buying experience, we want to let you know that your feedback means the world to us.

We would be extremely grateful if you could leave us a positive feedback with
5 stars service rating

Are you satisfied with the purchase?
- YES ★★★★★
- NO ★★★☆☆

Regards,

COLORMOOD Books

Our other books

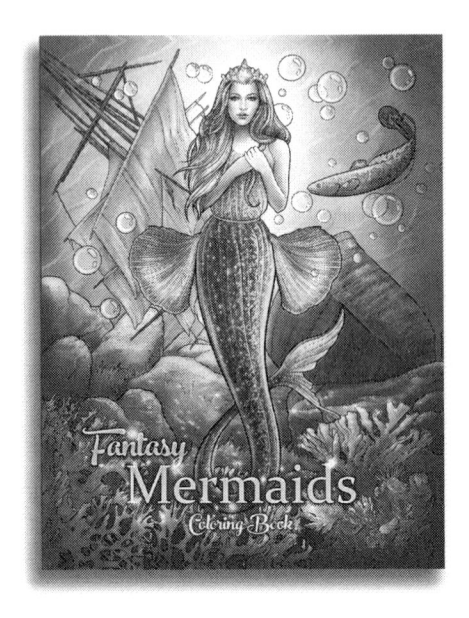

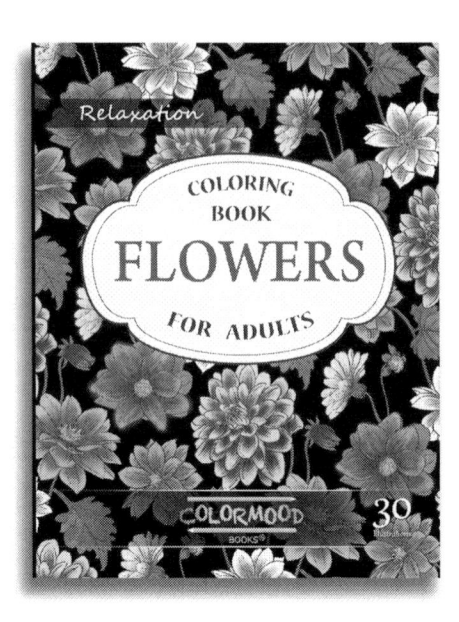

Fantasy Mermaids:

An Adult Coloring Book with Beautiful Mermaids, Underwater World and its Inhabitants, Detailed Designs for Relaxation (Stress Relief)

Beautiful Fairies and Elves:

Coloring Book For Experienced User (Stress Relief)

Flowers Coloring Book:

An Adult Coloring Book with Flower Collection, Stress Relieving Flower Designs for Relaxation

+ Follow

Help other colorists discover our artwork.
Post your work on Instagram and tag us @colormoodbooks

www.colormoodbooks.com
Email: info@colormoodbooks.com